TRAINING YOUR YOUR CREATIVE MIND

Arthur B. VanGundy, Ph.D.

PRENTICE-HALL, INC., Englewood Cliffs, N.J. 07632

To
Denilyn, Sarah, and Laura

Training Your Creative Mind
by Arthur B. VanGundy, Ph.D.
© 1982 by Arthur B. VanGundy, Ph.D.
Address inquiries to Prentice-Hall, Inc.,
Englewood Cliffs, N.J. 07632
Printed in the United States of America
Prentice-Hall International, Inc., London
Prentice-Hall of Australia, Pty. Ltd., Sydney
Prentice-Hall of Canada, Ltd., Toronto
Prentice-Hall of India Private Ltd., New Delhi
Prentice-Hall of Japan, Inc., Tokyo
Prentice-Hall of Southeast Asia Pte. Ltd., Singapore
Whitehall Books Limited, Wellington, New Zealand

10 9 8 7 6 5 4 3 2 1

ISBN 0-13-926717-4

ISBN 0-13-926709-3 {PBK}

Library of Congress Cataloging in Publication Data
VanGundy, Arthur B.
    Training your creative mind.

    Bibliography: p.
    Includes index.
        1. Creative ability—Problems, exercises, etc.
    2. Creative thinking—Problems, exercises, etc.
    I. Title
BF408.V25   153.3'5   81-22651
ISBN 0-13-926717-4   AACR2
ISBN 0-13-926709-3 (pbk.)

CONTENTS

PREFACE

Most books on creativity begin by noting that creativity has been a topic of considerable interest over the years (this book obviously is no different in this regard). For the last several decades hundreds of research studies have been conducted on creativity, and thousands of individuals, groups, and organizations have used formal creativity methods. There is little doubt that a large number of people have at least a passing interest in some form of creativity.

However, the degree of this interest has tended to wax and wane over the years. Like any management or self-improvement tool, creativity has been buffeted by the fickle winds of change as people bounce from one fad to another.

We seem to have embarked on a never-ending quest to better ourselves. We try first one tool and then another and another, all the while hoping that we'll eventually arrive at some ill-defined state of nirvana. We have become so inundated by advertising exhorting us to smell better, see better, feel better, become thinner, and gain more control of our lives that it makes you wonder how so many people have managed to survive without these self-improvement aids.

Although creativity also has been treated as a fad, it is one ability that we can't do without. Most of our personal accomplishments in life depend upon our creative skills. Because we all live in a constantly changing environment, we have learned that any progress we make (and sometimes our very survival) depends on our ability to develop new approaches to our problems. Although we always have been somewhat proficient at creative problem solving, the new demands imposed by our world require that we learn how to become even more proficient.

Similar sentiments have been reflected by many of our business and political leaders. Unfortunately, most of these sentiments amount to little more than giving lip service to satisfy what others may want to hear. When it comes to actually taking measures to improve creativity and innovation, very little activity can be observed. We like to see technological innovations and creative products, but when it comes to stimulating the development of these outcomes, not much has been accomplished. It would appear that we live in a society that applauds creativity but tends to look down on creativity methods and those who openly engage in creative thinking.

One way we can begin to alter this situation is by personally attempting to become more creative. Wouldn't it be nice if only 10 percent of the population could double their creative abilities? Think of all we could accomplish if this should happen. Many of the problems we now view as unsolvable might suddenly become solvable, more jobs might be produced, personal and corporate incomes might rise, and a greater number of people might find more fulfillment in their lives. Is all this a pipe dream? Perhaps. But unless we try new ways of dealing with our problems, they only will continue to proliferate and grow in intensity.

Many of the current books on creativity offer little concrete advice for people who sincerely want to become more creative. They may offer the expectation and hope of becoming more creative, but the means provided to achieve this goal often are not specified or are poorly defined. Reading about the nature of creativity and completing some creative-thinking exercises are not enough to induce growth in creative functioning.

Like anything we are committed to achieving, creative growth requires a planned and organized approach. However, this approach should not be too planned and organized. Some flexibility will be needed to deal with any obstacles that we may encounter. This is not to say that our approach should be hit or miss, either. We do need to have some method to our madness.

I have written this book to provide some method to my own madness. In this instance, my "madness" is to become more creative and to help other people do the same. Having read many books and articles on creativity during the past several years, and having conducted workshops and used creativity techniques in solving my own problems and those of others, I am now convinced that it is possible to grow creatively. I have no doubt about it. However, most of the books and articles I read on the subject were a continuing source of frustration. They offered little in the way of a systematic approach to becoming more creative. Instead, the primary focus in a lot of this literature has been on imparting knowledge and telling the reader what he or she should be doing to be creative. Although this information was extremely helpful, I still felt that something was missing.

This gap in my personal needs became more and more evident every time I ran across some creative-thinking exercises. Whether or not I could deal with these exercises to my own satisfaction no longer was of major importance to me. I felt that I only was getting bits and pices of a larger puzzle. The need to learn how to put it all together kept growing and growing. Finally, I decided that I would need to put together my own program. This book is the result of that effort.

This book was written for people who are seriously interested in becoming more creative. It was not written for people who only are interested in learning about what creativity is and what it can or cannot do. Instead, it is a program for correcting the imbalance that exists in most of our thinking processes.

For too long, most of us have neglected our creative minds in favor of our logical minds. Both thinking modes are important, but we have been trained throughout our lives to become more logical and analytical. If we can apply the same effort to training our creative sides, then we will be in a much better position to make optimal use of all our capabilities.

This book is directed primarily to persons with little prior exposure to creative thinking. Those persons who are fairly proficient creative thinkers may not find the same amount of value in the exercises as those who are less proficient. Nevertheless, everyone who is committed to becoming more creative should find that there are many areas in which they can receive some benefit.

In Chapter One I discuss the general nature of individual creativity, the human mind and brain, left and right brain functional distinctions, plus a few thoughts on training, types of problems, and general expectations. In Chapter Two I discuss thirty creative-thinking obstacles organized into five major categories: perceptual, emotional, intellectual/expressive, cultural, and environmental. I would suggest that you read this chapter at least twice, skimming over it the first time and then reading for understanding the second time. The more personal awareness you develop about these obstacles, the more likely it will be that you will benefit fully from the exercises. If you can, you might try to relate some personal problem to each one of the obstacles. In Chapter Three I go into some detail on preparing for your program and carrying it out. In this chapter I cover such topics as your mental attitude, the need for relaxation and some suggested relaxation methods, assessing your current level of creative thinking and your readiness to begin the program, a suggested program outline, and, finally, guidelines for evaluating and maintaining training performance.

In Chapters Four through Ten I present the seventy-five exercises that make up the core of your program. You will find exercises on problem preparation and awareness (Chapter 4), sensory awareness (Chapter 5), flexibility (Chapter 6), fluency (Chapter 7), originality (Chapter 8), solution evaluation and selection (Chapter 9), and gaining acceptance and planning for implementation (Chapter 10). In Chapter Eleven I describe the final phase of your program. In this chapter you are asked to apply your learnings from the previous chapters to a hypothetical and a personal problem of your choice. I sincerely hope that you will receive as much benefit from your program as I have from writing this book.

My thanks go to all the people in classes and seminars who have helped me refine many of the exercises with their participation and comments. I also am indebted to many of these people for their sample responses to many of the exercises. A special note of thanks goes to Dudley Lynch for helping to stimulate my interest in right-brain thinking. Finally, I would like to thank Lynn Crussel and Suzi Overstreet for their invaluable and expert assistance in typing major portions of the manuscript.

1

INTRODUCTION TO MIND TRAINING

What percent of the general population do you consider to be creative? Ten percent? Twenty? Thirty? Forty? Fifty percent or more? When I ask this question of participants in workshops and classes, most people select 20 percent or less as the correct figure. Their reasoning seems to be that creativity, like intelligence and other personality attributes, is a trait that is normally distributed throughout the population. That is, most people are "average" in creativity, while only a small percentage can be considered "truly" creative or noncreative.

If this reasoning is correct, what is it that separates the average from the highly creative person? Why, for example, are such persons as da Vinci, Franklin, and Einstein regarded as creative while others are not? Are the differences hereditary? Or are environmental, social, or cultural factors more involved? Aren't all people created equal? Although the answers to these and similar questions have been the subject of considerable debate over the years, one thing is fairly certain: *All of us are creative; we vary only in the extent to which we have developed our creativity potential.*

Thus, in answer to the question I posed earlier, 100 percent of people in the general population are creative. The only way most of us differ from those whom we consider to be creative geniuses is that these latter individuals somehow have managed to grasp the meaning and significance of their creativeness. And they have been able to direct this creativeness into channels that bring recognition to their creative achievements. Through some combination of personal factors and environmental circumstances, they have learned how to maximize the innate creative potential possessed by us all.

Although most of us have learned how to be logical and analytical, only a few of us have learned how to use our inborn intuitive and creative capabilities. The key, then, to making optimal use of our creativity potential is *learning how to unlock the creative side of our brain*—not the analytical side, since we have already done a pretty good job of that.

Our creative minds were not always locked. As children we all were capable of developing insights and ideas which, if polished by experience and technical knowledge, might be recognized as creative if proposed by an adult. Yet somewhere between childhood and adulthood, our creative minds began to atrophy until we no longer could rely on this aspect of our thinking process to express ourselves creatively.

An analogy can be made with a weight lifter who concentrates on building strength in the left arm while neglecting the right. Over time, the left arm will develop a disproportionate amount of strength, far exceeding that of the right. As Socrates once noted, "That which is used strengthens and grows, while that which is not used withers and dies."

So too it is with our creative minds. We must exercise *both* sides of our minds to become fully functioning human beings. It would be folly to think that we could ever become complete as persons by strengthening only our analytical minds. Yet many of us have allowed our creative selves to slowly wither. As a consequence, we are not expressing ourselves and growing as people to the extent that we are capable.

Although it would be easy to blame various institutions—such as the schools—for this loss of our creativity, the actual cause is probably much more complex. In all likelihood, the fault lies with our society and its cultural values and mores, which too often stress conformity and rationality while relegating independence of thought and creativity to less-important roles.

Whatever the reason, the fact remains that many of us are searching for ways to awaken our creative selves and grow to all that we are capable of being. Analytical skills also are important for human functioning and development, but are often overused and misused. Learning how to use the neglected side of our brain, the creative side, can provide the balance so essential to optimal functioning and growth.

THE HUMAN MIND AND BRAIN

Before we can think about unlocking our creative minds, it is necessary to understand how the mind and the brain differ. They often are used as synonymous terms, but it may not always be appropriate to do so. In fact, a rather strict distinction can be made between the mind and the brain, especially in terms of how they function.

The human mind generally is considered to be the center of all mental activity. It is through the mind that we reason, learn, perceive, judge, feel, and perform all the other activities associated with mental functioning. The mind gives meaning to life and enables us to understand and deal with the world around us.

The mind is an intangible concept. We cannot touch it. We only seem to know that it is there (except, of course, when we "lose" our minds!) Nevertheless, we must have a mind to know that it is there. The proof of its existence lies in its existence. I think; therefore I am.

Because the mind is intangible, it is difficult to subject it to scientific scrutiny. The mind cannot be measured or weighed, and it is almost (if not) impossible to test for its effect on other things. Perhaps we can test it philosophically, but we cannot test it from a scientific standpoint since there is no valid way to measure the scientific existence of the mind and its nature and composition.

The human brain, in contrast, can be scientifically investigated. It is an anatomical part of the body that possesses size, shape, texture, color, weight, and structure. Its effect on other things can be studied, and alternative hypotheses can be developed and scientifically tested to explain the existence or nonexistence of its effect. A lesion can be made in the occipital lobe of the brain, for example, and observed for its effect on vision. Lesions then can be made on the other portions of the brain and if no effect on vision is noticed, then it can be concluded that the occipital lobe alone is concerned with vision. No similar types of experiments can be conducted on the mind with the same degree of scientific precision.

Nevertheless, the mind does depend on the physical structures of the brain for its existence. In this sense, the brain can be regarded as the instrument of the mind. It provides the organization and connections among the different brain areas that permit discussion of the mind as a concept. However, the mind is still a philosophical or psychological concept, not a physiological one.

The human brain, as we know it, is thought to have

evolved from three different forms. The first form was the reptilian brain, containing the brain stem and neural fibers organized to deal with routine situations. This brain form was concerned with such basic responses as territoriality and imitation. Although still with us, the reptilian brain is not very helpful in making adaptations and dealing with novel situations. The second brain form is known as the mammalian brain. As it evolved, it became integrated with and surrounded the reptilian brain. With this brain we became more adept at such actions as learning, expressing emotions, sensing, and responding to environmental changes. It is from this brain that we developed the fight-or-flight response to stressful situations. In contrast to the two previous brain systems, which integrated their functions, the third brain form—the neocortex—has retained a separate identity. It has provided us with such abilities as speaking, thinking, walking, using symbols, and creating. With this brain, further evolutionary forms may not be necessary. We now are capable of solving problems. And with this ability we can learn to deal with or adapt to most situations we encounter.

However, very little is known about how the brain helps us to solve problems. We do know that a considerable amount of neuronal activity is involved, and that this activity takes place at an extremely rapid rate—much like a computer or a telephone-switching network. Yet many of the specific chemical processes and centers related to problem solving have continued to elude us. Perhaps, as is often noted, we are limited in our ability to study the brain since the brain itself is the major tool we have with which to study.

TWO BRAINS ARE BETTER THAN ONE

Most people probably are unaware that the human brain is actually two brains in one, consisting of a left and a right hemisphere. The hemispheres are symmetrical in shape, but not in function. The left hemisphere controls the right side of the body, while the right hemisphere controls the left side. As much research has demonstrated, an injury to one hemisphere affects the opposite side of the body. Thus, if the left hemisphere is damaged, the ability to use our right arm, for example, will be seriously impaired.

This distinction between the two hemispheres has been recognized for many years. What is relatively new, however, is the knowledge of the roles the hemispheres play in our mental processes. In particular, the differentiated aspects of the brain halves determine how we use our minds. The left hemisphere is concerned primarily with verbal skills and words, while the right hemisphere is concerned with sensory images. In addition, the left half tends to think in a logical and sequential manner, processing only one bit of information at a time. The right half, in contrast, is more intuitive, processes information that cannot be put into words, thinks in terms of whole patterns even when only partial information is available, and is unconcerned with the order in which thinking occurs. A more complete listing of these and other hemispherical differences is shown in Figure 1.1.

Figure 1.1 Comparison of Left and Right Brain Hemispheres

Left Brain	Right Brain
logical	intuitive
sequential	nonsequential
analytical	nonanalytical
rational	emotional
uses words	uses images
systematic	disorderly
intellectual	experiential
literal meanings	metaphorical meanings
objective	subjective
judgmental	nonjudgmental
requires all data	uses incomplete data
realistic	fantasy-like
verbal relations	spatial relations
part-by-part analysis	holistic analysis

The importance of these functional distinctions to creative thought cannot be minimized. Because creative thinking involves manipulation of both words and images, we can never maximize our creative potential if we limit ourselves to only one way of thinking. Creative thinking requires the use of both thinking modes—only at different times during the thinking process. Specifically, the right brain helps us avoid rigid, linear thinking so that we can concentrate on developing ideas, while the left brain helps us to evaluate these ideas and test them against reality.

Most of the knowledge we have acquired is the result of the left brain's ability to translate creative insights into words. Words are the symbols we use to communicate and understand ideas. Most creative breakthroughs, however, were not developed through the singular use of verbal and analytical thinking. Instead, most creative insights evolved from the right brain's ability to image and construct whole patterns and spatial relationships. For example, Albert Einstein has described how his thought processes involved two different stages. In the first stage he usually played with different combinations of problem elements—without regard to any logical patterning of the elements. In this stage he relied primarily upon his right brain. The second stage involved use of the left brain to translate his final solution into conventional words or symbols. Given the magnitude of his achievements, Einstein appears to have made optimal use of both his brain hemispheres.

The lesson, then, is that both brain hemispheres need to work in harmony if we are to produce creative solutions to our problems. There are times when the left brain must remain idle while the right brain does its thing. The reverse also is true: There are times when the strengths of the left brain must be used. For most of us, achieving a balance between our right and left brains is not just a simple matter of switching to the appropriate hemisphere. We need, instead, to learn how to awaken our largely unused right brain.

TRAINING YOUR MIND

Developing this creative side of ourselves requires training. Just as athletes must train and condition their bodies, so must we exercise and condition our minds. We must continually work on the ability to confront and deal with the day-to-day problems we face; to strengthen our weak areas and refine and upgrade our strong areas. In short, we need to practice using the mental skills required for growth and survival as human beings.

In one respect, we receive practice in these skills every day. We constantly are challenged by events that exercise both our creative and analytical minds. Whether writing a paper, balancing a budget, or interacting with other people, we are using both sides of our brains to some extent. Unfortunately, most of this practice uses the left brain more than the right, since the left brain has become our dominant thinking mode. In addition, the majority of the practice we receive is hit or miss. For most of us there is nothing systematic about the way we acquire analytical and creative skills.

Although we cannot expect to receive systematic practice in thinking skills through everyday living, it is possible to become more focused in our approach. For example, by being aware of what thinking mode is best for a situation, we can practice applying the appropriate skills. Thus, if a task involves developing a new program, project, or plan of some sort, we can begin by concentrating on visual images and patterns of relationships while suspending all logical thinking. Then, once we have crystallized our approach, we can apply the critical censors of the left brain to evaluate the result. In this manner, we are making a conscious attempt to involve the right brain while simultaneously learning how to integrate it with the left.

Another way we can become more disciplined in our approach is through practice exercises specifically geared to aspects of left- and right-brain functioning. However, since the left brain tends to be dominant in most of us, it probably is best to begin with exercises designed to strengthen and develop our creative minds. We usually need to build up our right brains first to combat the often overpowering influence of our left brains. Then, once we have learned to apply right-brain thinking, we can work on integrating it with the left brain.

Nevertheless, the approach we use for right-brain development will need to be somewhat systematic. And, because of our limited use of the right brain, we cannot immediately begin with complex right-brain types of exercises any more than we can run a marathon without prior training. We must start out slowly and gradually experience different types and intensities of right-brain functioning. In addition, we have to adapt our training program to our needs and constraints. More will be said on these considerations in the following chapters.

KNOW YOUR PROBLEMS

Most human activity involves problem solving. And problem solving requires use of both logical and creative thinking modes. It then follows that anything we can do to increase our thinking capabilities should help us to become better problem solvers and, ultimately, more well-rounded individuals.

Problems vary, however, in the type of thinking needed to solve them. Although it is an oversimplification, it can be said that structured problems require mostly left-brain thinking while unstructured problems require mostly right-brain thinking. Because this book is concerned with developing the creative mind, the underlying objective of your training program will be to increase your ability to solve unstructured types of problems. This is not to say that other types of problems are not important. It just happens that creative thinking is most economically and effectively used when it is applied to unstructured problems.

The problems we encounter in our daily lives run the gamut from highly structured to highly unstructured. Most structured problems, such as assembling a bicycle, require relatively routine responses based on analytical types of thinking. These types of problems are distinctive in that it is usually pretty clear how to solve them, and it is easy to determine if they have been solved. Unstructured problems, in contrast, provide few guidelines on how to go about solving them; typically, there is no way to evaluate the correctness of any proposed solutions. A problem involving ways to reduce energy consumption, for example, is unstructured: No recipe exists on the best way to go about reducing consumption and, more important, there is no guarantee that any action taken will be successful in resolving the problem. Such problems require a highly developed creative mind, one that cannot hope to be successful by relying only on judgment and logical thinking.

EXPECTATIONS

Usually when we begin anything new, we have a general set of expectations about what we hope to accomplish. You no doubt have some expectations about how you will be different after completing the program outlined in this book. Some of these expectations may be realistic and some may be unrealistic. In addition, I have expectations for what I hope you will achieve. Again, some of these may be realistic and some may be unrealistic. Nevertheless, it is important that we all are aware of the objectives we have set for ourselves. Such objectives, in large part, will determine how much benefit we derive from what we attempt. If you have not yet assessed your expectations, you might want to do so now, before proceeding any further.

My personal expectations for you are that you will develop greater awareness of the power residing in your right brain and that you will develop the ability to apply this power appropriately to the problems you face. Furthermore, I expect that as you begin to exercise your creative mind, you eventually will do so as naturally and as easily as most of us have done with our analytical minds.

Of course, whether you do or not largely will be up to you. Just reading this book will not be enough. You will have to experience and understand the exercises presented and not just go through the motions. You also will have to commit yourself to applying what you learn so that you can draw upon both of your brains automatically. Without such a commitment, your left brain may resume dominance and prevent your right brain from doing all that it can do for you. The decision is yours.

Beyond these general considerations, I also have a set of specific objectives for you to achieve. In particular, after you have finished your training program, you should find that your thinking ability has improved in four major creativity areas: 1) problem sensitivity, 2) flexibility, 3) fluency, and 4) originality. Problem sensitivity refers to your ability to tune in to your problems, to be aware of all their various aspects and how they are related to one another. Flexibility is a skill involving the ability to break away from conventional problem constraints, to test surface assumptions, and to develop new problem perspectives. The ability to generate a large number of ideas and to see different associations and patterns are the primary aspects involved in fluency. Finally, originality deals with the uniqueness of the ideas you generate. Although the exercises in the following chapters cover many other related areas, these four will be of most value to you in developing your creative mind.

One final note before you begin: Although all our creative minds need some training, our analytical minds should not be neglected either. As mentioned previously, effective problem solving requires both types of thinking. Analyzing problem information and evaluating ideas, for example, requires a certain degree of judgmental and analytical thinking. For this reason, several of the exercises emphasize the use of analytical skills along with those designed to increase creative thinking. The major emphasis, however, will be on development of your creative mind.

OBSTACLES TO CREATIVE THINKING

When I was in high school I made several attempts at being an athlete. One of these attempts involved two years of running the high hurdles for the track team. I never did very well, being hampered by a lack of speed. My form in going over the hurdles, however, was excellent. As a result, I looked better than most of the other hurdlers when running a race. Unfortunately, the races weren't judged on who had the best form. (A relatively minor detail, in my opinion!).

Why do I chance boring you with this little tale from my past? The reason is that running the hurdles is a perfect analogy for introducing the topic of overcoming obstacles to creative thinking.

From my story, the most obvious analogy is that we

all must learn to accept our limitations whenever we encounter an obstacle we can't overcome. In this case, I could run only so fast, no matter how hard I worked at it. Moreover, I couldn't be judged on style, so I had to accept this limitation. In running the hurdles, as well as in creative thinking, we need to accept obstacles from within ourselves in addition to those imposed on us externally.

Another analogy between hurdling and overcoming creative-thinking obstacles also can be made. In hurdling, the obstacles (hurdles) are set out in front of you, waiting to be overcome. The same is true for creative thinking: the obstacles are there; it is up to you to overcome them.

When the actions involved in training for each are analyzed, the analogy becomes more obvious. Training for the hurdles involves first practicing your form by jumping over a few hurdles. Then, once you have mastered your form (assuming you already are in the proper physical condition), you must learn how to run over the hurdles, not jump over them. To do this requires a heavy emphasis on the right brain. The actions involved must be visualized and practiced until they become almost automatic. The result should be development of the flow and rhythm needed to successfully clear all the hurdles. Overcoming creative-thinking obstacles involves a similar set of activities. After you have identified the obstacles, you need to practice your "form" in clearing them. In this instance, form consists of the mental attitudes and skills needed to overcome each of the different obstacles that you may face. Running over the thinking obstacles comes next. To be effective, you will have to develop a flow and rhythm for dealing with each obstacle as you encounter it. And, like hurdling, overcoming creative-thinking obstacles requires adjustments in your flow and pace for each obstacle, depending upon the extent to which you already have overcome the obstacle. Thus, when you develop your own training program (described in Chapter 3), the style and form you use to run the "creativity race" probably will be considerably different from that used by other people. Because we all are so different in many ways, we have to spend some time learning which specific obstacles are preventing us from becoming more creative and how we can overcome them.

Why is it important to consider such matters? Why not just learn to use a large number of creativity techniques and apply them to our problems? Well, why not? There's really nothing wrong with using creative problem-solving techniques. If appropriately applied, they can produce large numbers of creative solutions. In fact, repeated use of many techniques can help in overcoming many creativity obstacles. The problem is that the flow and rhythm needed to automatically run over these obstacles is never completely internalized through the sole application of idea-generation methods. We need, instead, to create within ourselves a climate that allows us to deal easily with obstacles on a continuing basis. Short-term, one-shot attempts at overcoming obstacles will never permit us to develop the Olympian skills we require to become creativity athletes.

WHAT ARE THE CREATIVE-THINKING OBSTACLES?

Quite a few writers have identified a large number of obstacles that act as barriers to the emergence of right-brain thinking. I have pulled together thirty of these obstacles and organized them into the five major categories typically used to describe them: perceptual, emotional, cultural, environmental, and intellectual/expressive. The specific obstacles within each of these categories are presented in Figure 2.1.

Figure 2.1 Creative Thinking Obstacles

Perceptual Obstacles

    1. Using overly-restrictive problem boundaries.
    2. Inability to isolate the problem.
    3. Ignoring familiar sensory inputs (saturation).

    4. Stereotyping.
    5. Functional myopia.
    6. Failure to use all the senses.
    7. Difficulty in seeing remote relationships.

Emotional Obstacles

    1. Feeling overwhelmed by the problem.
    2. Fear of failure.
    3. Fear of criticism.
    4. Fear of taking a risk.
    5. Desire to succeed too quickly.
    6. Low tolerance of ambiguity.
    7. Failure to incubate.
    8. Failure to suspend judgment.

Intellectual/Expressive Obstacles

    1. Failure to use an appropriate problem solving language.
    2. Use of rigid problem solving strategies.
    3. Lack of information or use of incorrect information.

Cultural Obstacles

    1. Taboos.
    2. Tradition.
    3. Lack of a questioning attitude.
    4. Over-emphasis on competition or cooperation.
    5. Over-emphasis on reason and logic.
    6. Belief that fantasy and intuition are a waste of time.
    7. Lack of humor.

Environmental Obstacles

    1. Lack of time.
    2. Lack of support.
    3. Distractions.
    4. Autocratic bosses.
    5. Over-reliance on experts.

There is no particular order involved in this presentation, as we all are affected differently by the obstacles.

Like all such categorizations, there will be considerable overlap among the categories and, in many cases, an obstacle could have been just as easily placed in another category. Nevertheless, the use of categories provides a convenient format for learning about and understanding the obstacles.

In general, the obstacles can be classified as being either internal or external. Internal obstacles are those barriers that we impose on ourselves or have internalized as a result of our developmental experiences. To some extent, heredity also may play a role in the emergence of internal obstacles, although this is a controversial issue. The external obstacles are those that exist outside of ourselves—outside of our minds, if you will. However, these obstacles still are very real, since we perceive them with our minds. In fact, the actual difference between an internal and external obstacle may be an artificial distinction more appropriately discussed by philosophers.

The difference between internal and external obstacles might be more easily understood by attempting to describe their interrelationships visually (a right-brain activity). Such an attempt is shown in Figure 2.2.

At the core of the figure are the three categories of internal obstacles: perceptual, emotional, and intellectual/expressive. Each of these categories strongly overlaps the others, suggesting a high degree of interdependence and commonality. Intellectual functioning, for example, will be strongly affected by the emotional state of the mind.

This core is an immediate subset of the environmental obstacles which, in turn, are a subset of the cultural obstacles. Just as there is interdependency among the internal obstacles, so is there a certain amount of interdependency among the environmental and cultural obstacles. However, there are very few areas of commonality among the external obstacles. Cultural and environmental obstacles are rela-

Figure 2.2 Internal and External Creative Thinking Obstacles

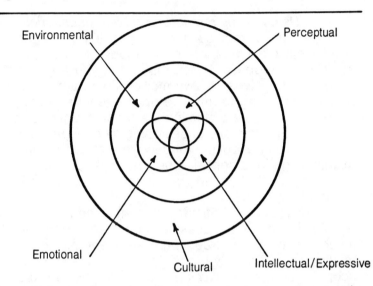

Environmental

Perceptual

Emotional

Cultural

Intellectual/Expressive

tively independent of one another, but are not mutually exclusive. That is, the transactions that take place between culture and environment are not so strong as to define common areas, but the transactions do occur.

Finally, it should be noted that the number and strength of interactions among the categories will be greater within the internal obstacles *or* between the internal and external obstacles. Perhaps a simpler way of saying this is that the obstacles within you are the major barriers to creative thinking that you face. Overcome these obstacles and the external ones will be much easier to handle. You will have liberated your mind and set the stage for unleashing your creative potential. You still will have to deal with the external obstacles, but you will have more self-awareness and control over the events in your creative life.

Given this conceptual background, I now will discuss the obstacles in greater detail.

PERCEPTUAL OBSTACLES

1. *Using overly restrictive problem boundaries.* This obstacle arises from our tendency to impose too many constraints on a problem or to impose constraints that don't exist. Suppose, for example, that you are trying to develop a new type of lawn mower. If you approach this problem by trying to improve upon a conventional lawn mower, you may be restricting the problem unnecessarily. Is the real problem one of designing a new type of mower, or should you be looking for new ways of cutting grass or maintaining it at a specified height? Perhaps the solution lies in chemically treating grass to retard its growth beyond a certain level.

The lesson is that many problems need to be broadened to overcome unnecessary constraints. However, the reverse also can be true. There are many problems that may be unnecessarily broad and need to be reduced in scope. Thus, if you are a manufacturer of lawn mowers, you may be restricted to nonchemical solutions due to the constraints imposed by your available technology and equipment. In any event, a clear understanding of problem boundaries is essential for effective problem solving.

2. *Inability to isolate the problem.* Overcoming this obstacle is important for helping us to avoid correctly solving the wrong problem or incorrectly solving the right problem. That is, we must be certain that we are dealing with the real problem and not just what appears to be the problem. If your car doesn't start in the morning, then you might want to check the gas tank before you begin taking apart the carburetor (correctly solving the wrong problem). You also don't want to fill the gas tank with milk to get the car started (incorrectly solving the right problem). To avoid both of these situations, the problem must be adequately defined before attempting any solution.

3. *Ignoring familiar sensory inputs (saturation).* Without looking, draw the face of your watch (if you don't have a watch, draw a telephone dial with all the letters and

numbers in their correct place). Most people have trouble doing either one of these tasks correctly. To avoid becoming overloaded with minutiae, the mind only retains such data for a relatively short period of time. It subconsciously ignores most data that have become familiar sights. In effect, the mind becomes saturated with familiar sensory inputs and no longer recognizes them as novel stimuli. Although this function of the mind serves a useful purpose in preventing us from being overwhelmed by unnecessary data, it can be a disadvantage when it comes to creative thinking. To be creative, we need new and unique perspectives; we need to look at the world with a fresh eye and to open up all our senses. We can't get such perspectives, however, if the familiar things in our lives are always sensed in the same way.

4. *Stereotyping.* Stereotyping acts as a block to creative thinking whenever we tend to see what we expect to see. To some extent, all of us engage in this type of behavior. We disregard many facts or reinterpret them to conform with our preconceived beliefs. If we want to believe something or have been conditioned to believe it, then we usually will persist in believing it to be so even when there is little evidence to support our beliefs.

This way of viewing the world can help us to deal with many ambiguous situations. Specifically, it allows us to create order out of chaos.

Stereotyping, however, is not very conducive to creative thinking. Once we affix a label, it is very hard to remove it and develop a new perspective. For example, many people may find themselves lacking a screwdriver to repair some mechanical device and give up in frustration. Had they not stereotyped the coins in their pockets as money, they might have thought of using them to solve the problem. Or, for a more personal example, think of the different ways people have stereotyped you. It is unfortunate that so many human resources go unused because of the stereotyping that we all engage in.

Equally unfortunate is the tendency to stereotype

certain problems as being similar. This will occur whenever a problem is only superficially examined. How many times, for example, have you been faced with what appears to be a problem situation, only to discover later that it wasn't really a problem after all? An even more serious situation is encountered when trying to apply a solution that solved a problem in the past to one in the present. By stereotyping problems as similar, the danger exists that the same solution will not work for the new problem. In fact, transferring solutions in this manner can even make some problems more difficult to solve or create entirely new problems.

5. *Functional myopia.* This rather fancy-sounding obstacle is a psychological term used to describe the tendency of some people to select aspects of a problem related to the training they received in a particular discipline. For example, people in organizations usually describe organizational problems from the perspective of their department or work group. Thus, the assembly-line worker will be concerned with on-the-job worker needs, the personnel officer with recruiting and retaining personnel, and the financial officer with the flow of cash and other fiscal concerns. If you ask any one of these individuals what is the most pressing problem facing their company, they invariably will reply in terms of their own functional areas.

Such a response might be expected, given the highly specialized format of most bureaucracies. However, viewing a complex, unstructured problem (i.e., one with many interdependent parts) from only one perspective is not likely to produce a unique solution or one that will solve the problem. We need to ask ourselves, instead, how would someone else in another discipline solve this problem? Better yet, ask people from different areas for their opinion. If you do, you are likely to enrich your own knowledge and increase the odds of solving your problems.

6. *Failure to use all the senses.* We are continually bombarded by a variety of sensory inputs. We see images, hear sounds, feel textures, taste flavors, and smell odors every day. Rarely, however, do we make full use of all these

senses in solving our problems. We have become conditioned to using verbal skills (a left-brain activity) in understanding problem situations, but we tend to neglect the
other sensory experiences available to us.

Many businesses tend to capitalize on this obstacle.
Food-products manufacturers, for example, are very aware
of the need to use all the senses. For instance, can you
imagine buying a new type of margarine that contained
lumps, was purple in color, and tasted like turpentine?
Except for providing a unique sensory experience, such a
product offers no attraction. Yet, many of us fail to consider
how we can use our senses and how they are interrelated.

Effective problem solving requires that we experience our problems in as many ways as possible. We need
to open up more often the sensory grab bag that resides in
us all. Otherwise we will approach most problems from too
narrow a perspective to ever produce creative solutions.

7. *Difficulty in seeing remote relationships.* The ability to transfer a concept from one area to another is an
essential skill in creative problem solving. Because most
creative thought involves making connections between
apparently unrelated ideas, lack of this ability will result in
mundane, traditional solutions. To be creative, we must
learn to see the similarities and differences between objects or ideas that we normally would not see. If we use only
judgment and logic to get our ideas, we will restrict the
number of solution possibilities as well as limit the uniqueness of the final solution.

To illustrate the importance of seeing remote relationships, think of what associations wet leaves might have
with potato chips. Such an exercise can be hard to do
without having an actual problem to solve. However, a real
problem did exist that used this association to come up
with a solution. The problem involved developing a way to
make potato chips from dehydrated potatoes. The answer
was found by noting how leaves become easily com-
pressed when they are wet. By adding water and com-
pressing the dehydrated mixture, almost any form desired

can be produced—including that of a potato chip. Although this type of association might seem difficult to do, it is actually rather easy once the dominance of the left brain is overcome.

EMOTIONAL OBSTACLES

1. *Feeling overwhelmed by the problem.* This is a common obstacle experienced by most people who are unaccustomed to dealing with unstructured problems. Because such problems provide few guidelines on how to solve them and frequently are complex, with many subproblems, it is natural to feel that we may have bitten off more than we can chew. However, depending on our level of motivation and need to solve the problem, we must plunge in and do the best we can. A stiff upper lip and all that.

Yet, such an admonition is not likely to ease the stress felt from being overwhelmed or "problem heavy." A more realistic approach might be to develop a systematic process to break down the problem into more manageable units. In this way, the enormity of the problem won't be so overpowering. Another way of saying all of this is that before complex problems can be resolved, the problem of *how* to solve the problem must be dealt with first. Once this initial problem is resolved, the emotional obstacle presented by an originally overwhelming problem should be greatly diminished.

2. *Fear of failure.* Wouldn't it be nice if we could predict, with absolute accuracy, the outcome of every action we took? Obviously we can't, since usually there are many variables unknown to us or outside our control. Yet this unpredictable aspect of life seems to generate considerable anxiety among those who are determined to succeed at everything they do. Such individuals appear to overlook a basic fact of life: Most who have succeeded in life have done so with the *benefit* of many failures. They have learned to use their failures as stepping-stones to

success. Perhaps the greatest failure such people should worry about is failing to try.

This basic principle of failure is especially applicable to creative problem solving, where many unknowns must be confronted. These unknowns and the lack of certainty in outcomes involved in creative problem solving make it an area to be avoided by all who fear failure. However, once it is learned that failures in creativity can be beneficial, then there will be little to fear.

3. *Fear of criticism.* This obstacle has long been recognized as a common barrier to creative thinking. Although categorized as an emotional block, it also could be viewed as a cultural obstacle.

It almost seems to be a fundamental aspect of our culture to offer negative criticism whenever a new idea is proposed. Suggesting something new implies a possible disruption of the status quo, and for many people the idea of change is intolerable. The danger of this obstacle to creative thinking is that many people have been conditioned to expect criticism or tend to shy away from suggesting anything new or radical. Over the years, thousands of valuable ideas must have been lost to the world due just to this one obstacle.

Granted, not all ideas proposed will be winners. What most people tend to overlook, however, is that it only takes one good idea to make a difference. Unless the climate is created for the emergence of this idea, it will never stand a chance to be scrutinized. In addition, even if an idea is shown to have little merit, it may be that it will suggest a more useful idea to someone else, or possibly it could be combined with another idea to produce a workable solution.

4. *Fear of taking a risk.* In any endeavor, the safe course is the easy course. From childhood we have been taught to take it easy, to put safety first, to look before we leap. All of this advice is wise counsel. There are many situations in which we have to be careful not to jeopardize our lives, our careers, or our marriages, to name a few.

However, the easy course is not always the best course. Just because we must exercise caution in some of our activities doesn't mean that we need to avoid risk in all of our activities. This is especially true in creative problem solving, where many of the ideas proposed will present a risk to the proposer or those affected by the ideas. Of course, not all ideas will involve a risk. But even if a few do, the tendency to suggest something new often is suppressed as risk avoidance becomes a generalized attitude.

Typically, most feelings of risk avoidance exist due to an unrealistic assessment of the probable consequences of an idea. We become afraid to take a chance before we have even analyzed the things that could go wrong. When you look at this attitude rationally, it seems rather silly. Nevertheless, because we all are human, it is difficult to overcome such ingrained feelings. Perhaps the best we can do is become aware of when we tend to avoid risks, look at why we are afraid of them, and try to determine realistically any negative consequences involved. If we could adopt such an approach, we should find it much easier to separate generalized risk avoidance from fear of specific situations.

5. *Desire to succeed too quickly.* Most of us are concerned with doing our best. Whether we are interested in advancing in our jobs or just growing as persons, we strive to do most things to the best of our abilities. In our culture, this attitude is greatly reinforced and looked upon favorably. It is the way to get ahead.

However, there are times when we simply try too hard. In our attempt to give it "our all," we sometimes become too motivated and end up performing far below our actual capabilities. Remember when I discussed my hurdling career? Although I wasn't blessed with much speed, it took me quite a few races to realize that straining and hyping myself up for a race would not make me run faster. In fact, such behavior had the opposite effect: I became so tense that I actually ran slower than I was capable of doing. Once I learned this secret, I was able to increase my time over the hurdles so that I at least looked like I was running in fast slow motion.

The same type of overmotivated behavior can be detrimental to creative thinking. Leaping into problem-solving activity with the expectation of a quick solution is likely to produce just that. However, the quality and uniqueness of such a solution is not likely to be very high. Instead, time needs to be spent in analyzing the problem and in incubation—the unconscious digestion of ideas. Your left brain wants you to push for an immediate solution, but it is unlikely you will get a creative one unless you allow your right brain time to mull over and digest the problem.

6. *Low tolerance of ambiguity.* People who have trouble tolerating ambiguity or uncertainty generally tend to think in either-or terms and have a strong desire for closure. These individuals view the world and what happens in it as either being right or wrong, black or white. They have trouble seeing the gray areas that might exist in between. Thus, you are either smart or dumb, happy or sad, or a problem is either one thing or another. In addition, these people have a very strong need to restore order to a chaotic situation and can't tolerate disorder. In problem solving, these people want to rush right in and solve the problem without bothering to define the problem situation. For them, the solution is more important than the problem.

Like many of the other obstacles, there is nothing inherently wrong with having such a block to creative thinking. The ability to bring order out of chaos definitely has a place in our society. The difficulty arises when someone who is overly concerned with restoring order attempts to apply creative thinking to an unstructured problem. The fuzziness of such a problem usually is very frustrating to these individuals, and they are more likely to look for a quick fix or speedy solution than they are to spend time defining the problem. Problem solving does involve some elements of restoring order. An overemphasis on this, however, is unlikely to produce satisfactory results.

7. *Failure to incubate.* Incubation is, essentially, a

right-brain, unconscious, or preconscious activity that takes place following a period of intense concentration on a problem. It occurs whenever we leave a problem and do something unrelated to the problem. Then, when we least expect it, we are suddenly hit with a solution or another way of approaching the problem. This is the "aha" experience that frequently is reported by people who have developed creative insights to their problems.

In one respect, the failure to incubate is not really an emotional obstacle. We all are capable of incubating a problem. What is an obstacle to creative thinking is the failure to allow time for incubation when working on a problem. A problem can't be digested unless sufficient time is available. In some cases, all that may be needed is a twenty-minute break from the problem; in other instances, involving highly complex problems, several days or weeks may be needed.

8. *Failure to suspend judgment.* It is perhaps an unfortunate commentary on our society that we tend to place so much emphasis on negative criticism. The media and our educational institutions, to take just two examples, are notorious for the amount of effort they devote to critical and judgmental thinking. In fact, persons who excel at such thinking usually are rewarded for their ability to tear down the ideas of others. Although such an ability is necessary to advance knowledge, an overdose of it can be self-defeating.

Rejecting an idea as soon as it is proposed is similar to throwing away flower seeds because they are not very pretty. Of course, not all seeds will produce a beautiful flower. But unless they are given a chance, the result never will be known.

The tendency of many people to immediately squelch a new idea was clearly illustrated in a situation I once encountered with several of my colleagues. We proposed to some university officials that a need might exist for students to be exposed to creative thinking in addition to the heavy doses of analytical thinking they currently receive. We thought that one way to do this would be to develop a series of interdisciplinary courses that would draw upon specific fields to illustrate creative-thinking principles. From the response we received, it seemed as if we had just suggested that students be trained as Nazi storm troopers! The initial reaction went something like this: "Creative thinking can't be taught; it is something you either have or don't have [remember intolerance of ambiguity?]; if you have it, you need to develop it on your own; students are pigeonholes into which the university places knowledge; thinking is something each person must develop alone; besides, there aren't sufficient resources to maintain a new program." Not one positive feature of the proposal was considered by the officials.

While all of this was going on and we were discussing the problem of how to develop thinking skills in students, a colleague passed me a note that read: "I think we are talking to the problem."

If you don't want to become part of the problem, then you should look at your own behavior when new ideas are proposed. You always can criticize an idea later on, after it has had a chance to be considered or combined with another idea.

INTELLECTUAL/EXPRESSIVE OBSTACLES

1. *Failure to use appropriate problem-solving language.* This obstacle involves using the language of the left brain when right-brain language would be more appropriate, and vice versa. If you recall, the language of the left brain is basically verbal, while that of the right brain is more visual. Attempting to use verbal skills to solve a problem best dealt with by using visual skills would be inefficient and probably not produce a very satisfactory result. For example, if you are concerned with developing a new design for a car, verbal thinking alone would severely limit your

ability to come up with a creative product. The use of images would make such a task much easier.

Normally, the language we select to solve a problem is an unconscious decision resulting from prior trial-and-error approaches to similar problems. Perhaps more from habit than anything else, we make choices as to the best language form to use. And, because most of us are dominated by our left brains, the choices we make often turn out to be inappropriate. We need, instead, to begin making conscious choices about the problem-solving language that should be used.

As another illustration of the difference that can be achieved by using the appropriate language, consider the following problem:

All dogs have fur.
This animal has fur.
Therefore, it is a dog.

Some people will look quickly at this problem, verbally analyze it, and conclude that the last statement must be true. However, the validity of the statement easily can be rejected by using what is known as a Euler diagram. An example of such a diagram is shown in Figure 2.3. As

Figure 2.3 Example of a Euler Diagram

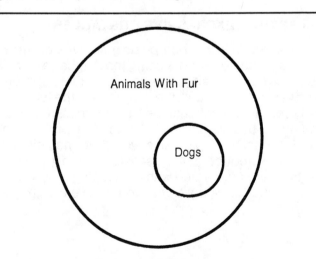

indicated by the drawing, dogs are only a subset of animals with fur. Therefore, the statement in the problem must be false. Although this problem also could have been solved using mathematical or verbal skills, it would have been inefficient to do so since the truth of the statement can be tested more easily using a simple diagram.

2. *Use of rigid problem-solving strategies.* This obstacle is very similar to the previous one. Its major premise is that we often become blocked by our inability to switch from one problem-solving process to another. For example, we might persist in trying to solve a problem using mathematics when no mathematical solution is possible (or feasible, given the limited knowledge most of us have about higher mathematics). An old riddle illustrates this point quite nicely:

> Farmer John told his three sons that when he died, they would all get a different proportion of the remaining horses on his farm. When he died, there were seventeen horses left. According to the will, the oldest son was to receive half the horses, the second son, a third of the horses, and the youngest son was to receive one ninth of the horses. The only stipulation was that none of the horses was to be killed to satisfy the requirements of the will. How was the will carried out?

If you tried to solve this problem using math, you probably didn't get very far. Based on conventional mathematical principles, a solution is impossible since there is no way that the requirements of the will can be satisfied as long as seventeen horses must be divided among the sons. Does this give you a clue as to how a solution might be found?

Two possible solutions are: 1) The brothers could pool their resources and buy another horse, which would permit fulfilling the stipulations in the will (the oldest son would receive nine horses, the second son six, and the youngest two), or 2) the brothers might take their problem to a rich judge, who might agree to buy another horse to satisfy the will. Both of these solutions are relatively simple and do not require use of a mathematical problem-solving strategy (other than to know that two, three, and nine are all evenly divisible into eighteen). In this case, persisting in the use of only one strategy would not have produced a very workable solution.

3. *Lack of information or use of incorrect information.* We've all heard the old saying that a little knowledge can be a dangerous thing. In many situations, we know a little about something and then try to apply this knowledge, only to find ourselves in over our heads. For example, we may know some of the basics about electrical systems, but end up frying ourselves when we try to wire a house for electricity.

Although there is some truth to this saying, it probably doesn't apply to all aspects of creative problem solving. To think creatively, it often is helpful if we have only a little information or knowledge about the problem we are trying to solve. If we have too much information, then we aren't very likely to develop new problem viewpoints; with just a little information, however, we won't be likely to use preconceived notions about how to produce solutions. Ideally, we will know just enough about the problem to play around with it in developing new perspectives, but not so much that we approach the problem with blinders on and focus only on one particular aspect of it.

An entirely different matter is when incorrect problem information is used. In this case, the amount of information is irrelevant, since only one erroneous bit of information can throw off the entire problem-solving process. And, if the incorrect information is gathered at the outset, it can be especially disastrous since such information often is used as the major standard for testing the validity of other bits of information. The assumptions behind all information gathered must be continually tested and refined to make sure that the "real" problem will be worked on.

CULTURAL OBSTACLES

1. *Taboos.* Taboos are standards imposed upon us by society that cause us to think or act in certain ways. Most taboos have a rational basis for their development in protecting members of society from harmful or unpleasant situations. For example, the Jewish taboo against eating pork originated at a time when cooking standards were not the same as they are today. By placing a negative sanction on pork, the Jewish people were protecting themselves from acquiring trichinosis.

Thus, there is nothing inherently wrong with taboos. A problem may exist, however, whenever taboos serve to restrict the range of possible solutions. If our culture does not permit something, then we will be less likely to consider using it in problem solving. This will be true even if a taboo is not likely to be violated. Awareness alone of a taboo often is enough to preclude its consideration.

2. *Tradition.* A certain sense of continuity and historical perspective on the way things are done probably is of value to any society. To live in the present, we sometimes have to understand a little about how things used to be. Living in the present also requires some perspective on how things might be. It was just such a future perspective that helped to forge the major achievements of modern societies.

Yet the past frequently is valued more than the future. Although it is nice to think of how things were, not much progress is likely to be made without some degree of a future orientation. Paradoxically, the same people who advocate change and innovation often are the ones who are reluctant to break away from established traditions. Most traditions are comfortable, secure, and certain, while most change is uncomfortable, threatening, and uncertain.

Many traditions are anathema to creative problem solving. In fact, tradition probably obscures the need for recognizing and dealing with many of the problems we should be confronting. Tradition also hobbles us as problem solvers when we try to gain acceptance for our ideas. Most creative solutions require some degree of change on the part of others, and it isn't likely to occur unless they also can break away from some of their traditions.

3. *Lack of a questioning attitude.* If you rarely ask questions, you rarely will risk looking stupid. You will risk, however, not growing as a person and learning about the world around you.

To be an effective problem solver requires knowledge, and a large proportion of our knowledge is obtained only through the use of questions. Unfortunately, many of us have suppressed our need to ask questions, since such behavior often is discouraged at a rather early age. Children are full of questions, but frequently find that adults aren't interested or don't have the time. As we grow up, we ask fewer and fewer questions, until we become reluctant to do so for fear that people will think we don't possess much knowledge. Yet we can't obtain knowledge unless we ask, ask, and ask some more.

In creative problem solving, a questioning attitude is essential for all aspects of the process. Facts continually need to be gathered about the problem, and many of these facts can be obtained only by asking questions. Thus, the more questions you ask about a problem, the more likely it is that you will be able to develop a satisfactory solution.

4. *Overemphasis on competition or cooperation.* Both competition and cooperation are healthy components of individual, group, and organizational functioning. Societal growth, as we know it, depends on getting along with others and trying to be first to get something done. As far as working with other people is concerned, there is very little that can be accomplished without some measure of each.

There is a danger, however, whenever we feel pressed to be too competitive or too cooperative. If we feel overly competitive in problem solving, then we may lose sight of the problem we are trying to solve. Instead, we may devote most of our energies to being the first to develop a solution for a solution's sake rather than an outcome that will be most effective in solving the problem. Too much emphasis on cooperation also can be damaging to effective problem solving behavior because of its effect on our motivation and creativity. If we continually are worried about not "rocking the boat" and not "stepping on toes," then we will be less likely to draw on our own uniqueness as creative problem solvers.

5. *Overemphasis on reason and logic.* Many people may find this obstacle too unrealistic. We have been trained to survive on reason and logic, and it can be difficult to see how it is ever possible to use too much of either. The difficulty is that reason and logic can't be used to solve all types of problems, or to help in all phases of the problem-solving process. Intuition and feeling can be equally valuable tools, by providing new ways of looking at problems and by assisting in the conceptualization of unique solutions. There is nothing wrong with reason and logic except that their overuse may tend to stifle many creative insights.

6. *Belief that fantasy and intuition are a waste of time.* This obstacle is closely related to the previous one in that our culture has conditioned us to believe in the power of one particular mode of thinking. Most of us are fact oriented in all of our activities and consider anything less to be nonproductive.

However, we can't be busy doing something concrete all of the time. There are situations in which we must speculate and daydream to allow our right brain to mull over a problem. Obviously, our fantasy adventures must be brought down to reality eventually, but as long as we are engaged in working on the problem, there can be no waste of time. If many of our ancestors had been restrained from fantasy activities, we would be without most of our current technological achievements. For example, how many people do you suppose spent "idle" time trying to figure out how humans could fly like birds? If these individuals had been restricted, we would be spending a lot more time today in traveling.

7. *Lack of humor.* Many aspects of human behavior can be characterized in terms of tension buildup and release. All physical, spiritual, and emotional forms of behavior make use of these actions to one extent or another. The outcome generally is a synthesis of a previous state of affairs or restoration of a state of equilibrium.

Problem solving also is characterized by tension buildup and release. Tension exists when a problem solver is first confronted with an unknown mess identified as a problem. The tension then increases or decreases in accordance with the problem solver's perception of progress toward problem resolution. Once the problem is resolved or accepted, tension is released, so that a tolerable threshold is created. That is, the problem may still be a mess, but the tension level associated with the mess is now acceptable.

Viewed in this way, problem solving is a serious business. When the process is couched in academic terms, there is very little leeway for straying from the single-minded goal of developing a solution. Frivolity may be considered extraneous to the whole process and not to be tolerated.

Unfortunately, such an attitude probably stifles more creativity than it helps. Humor is one form of release that can promote creative thinking. When working on a problem in a logical manner, it often takes a humorous insight involving an illogical concept to stimulate a potential solution. By laughing, we can unlock some of our rigid thinking patterns and view the problem in new ways. Humor, as found in most creative groups, is an excellent way to break out of mental ruts and conceptualize problems from different viewpoints. Although too much humor can be detrimental, a balanced amount always should be encouraged, whether in groups or working alone.

ENVIRONMENTAL OBSTACLES

1. *Lack of time.* This obstacle is pretty much self-explanatory. Developing creative solutions to unstructured problems can require considerably more time than is typically required of structured problems where routine procedures are available. As one of the resources needed to solve any problem, time can be a serious constraint.

However, it also can work to the benefit of the problem solver. There is some research evidence that having a deadline to work toward actually may increase the creativity of the solutions produced. Although this will not be true for all problems, a deadline can stimulate the development of more and higher-quality solutions. Nevertheless, most problem solvers would be wise to abide by the words of Henry Ford, who said, "The more you think, the more time you have."

2. *Lack of support.* The absence of any form of support—whether physical, monetary, emotional, or moral—can inhibit creative thinking. The creation of anything new typically is difficult whenever there is a lack of any form of support. At the very least, support can provide the minimal conditions needed to effectively conceptualize. An even more severe situation exists when attempting to put ideas into action. During this phase of the problem-solving process, support is critical to effective implementation. Without it, all creative efforts will be wasted.

3. *Distractions.* Have there been times when you wished you were a hermit? Did these times happen to coincide with a problem you were trying to solve? If so, then you probably were being bothered by one or more of the many distractions we all have to deal with every day. Phone calls, other people, noises, smells, sights, and the temperature all are factors that can disrupt our concentration.

Some people are more effective than others in shutting out these distractions. They somehow have learned how to "turn off their ears," as one of my young daughters is fond of saying. On the other hand, some distractions might be helpful in problem solving if they are used as sources of stimulation. For example, a chemist working on a new drug might use a ringing telephone to suggest development of a new type of time-release capsule. Of course, once the stimulation has been achieved, further ringing may be only another distraction to be eliminated.

4. *Autocratic bosses.* Most bosses have the ability to set the tone for the workers. This tone may be one of cooperation, competition, achievement, conflict, participation, mistrust, or any other of a number of environmental forces.

Bosses also play a critical role in the stimulation of imagination and creative thinking. Especially at the top levels of an organization, the amount of emphasis placed on creativity usually will filter downward through the different organizational levels. If the head honcho stresses freedom of thought, then this attitude is likely to be encouraged and transmitted to others; if creative thought is only given lip service, then it is not likely to be observed to any great extent.

The amount of emphasis placed on creative thinking probably varies with the personalities of the different bosses and with the structure, size, goals, and objectives of the organization. In addition, not all organizations will need or should have a highly creative atmosphere at all levels. Some activities must be routine for their efficient accomplishment. This is not to say that creativity should be suppressed. It should, instead, be managed by the bosses just as they manage any other organizational resource.

Unfortunately, many bosses have a severe case of "imarightitis," the belief that they always are right and that their conceptual skills are all that are needed to solve organizational problems. What these bosses fail to realize is that if they couple their creative skills with those of their subordinates, they will maximize the use of their human resources and solve more problems at the same time.

5. *Overreliance on experts.* It often has been said that an expert is anyone who lives more than one hundred miles from you and gives advice. Someone from the outside frequently is viewed as having more credibility than known personnel simply because he or she is from the outside.

There is nothing wrong with consulting an outside expert, since a fresh perspective on a problem can lead to many creative insights. The danger is in accepting expert opinion at face value. "Leave it to the expert" or "it must be true since the expert says it is" are commonly held attitudes about many experts. What many people fail to consider is that a lot of the knowledge possessed by experts results from a synthesis and personal interpretation of known facts or thought-to-be-known facts.

If we rely upon experts too heavily and accept their knowledge without questioning it, we are not likely to improve our own conceptual skills very much. It is so easy to depend upon others to solve our problems—and there is nothing wrong with seeking advice from time to time. We must learn, however, to distinguish fact from opinion and to question the assumptions and motivations of anyone who professes to be an expert. This caveat is especially true for experts who venture outside their field of specialization.

OVERCOMING CREATIVE-THINKING OBSTACLES

Many of the obstacles outlined in the previous section can be at least partially overcome by developing and using the personal training program described in the next chapters. Other obstacles simply will have to be accepted and tolerated. In an imperfect world we can't expect to have the ideal conditions to satisfy all our needs.

Nevertheless, there are specific actions we can take and attitudes we can develop to lessen the effect of many of the obstacles. Some of these actions will be easier for some people than for others, depending upon differences in motivation and prior knowledge of personal obstacles.

We all vary considerably in the nature and extent of our creativity blocks.

We need to develop an awareness of which specific obstacles we face as individuals, and then assess which ones we can and want to overcome. This is not an easy task, since we are not always aware of how or when we became blocked in problem solving. If you think that your personal-awareness level in this area is a little low, review the description of the different blocks and try thinking about some problem you are trying to solve. After you have worked on it for a while or have resolved it, think back on which obstacles you encountered, which ones you were not able to overcome, how you might better deal with them the next time, and why you had trouble with them. Make the effort to write down your thoughts and feelings. If you do this for several different types of problems, your obstacle awareness should increase substantially.

Here are some specific actions and attitudes you might consider in overcoming the obstacles:

Perceptual Obstacles

1. Avoid placing unnecessary constraints on the problem; always test all assumptions about problem boundaries.
2. Search for and isolate the real problem you want to solve.
3. Try to find a different way of viewing the problem; if possible, use a different sense than you normally would for the problem.
4. Avoid stereotyping the problem; be cautious in prematurely assigning a label to it.
5. Think of how someone in another discipline might try to solve the problem; consult with others from different disciplines for their perceptions of the problem.
6. Experience the problem as much as possible; consider how you might be able to see, touch, smell, hear, or taste the problem.

7. Practice associating unrelated objects or ideas to the problem, looking for similarities and differences.

Emotional Obstacles

1. Break down complex problems into manageable units; work on only one unit at a time.
2. Recognize that all people must fail sometimes before they can succeed. We grow only through learning from our failures.
3. Because we are unique, all of our ideas have value. Learn to expect criticism of your ideas and keep an open mind.
4. Be prepared to give up a little to get a little. Try to determine the probable negative consequences of any action involving risk and weigh these consequences against the alternative of no action.
5. Practice using patience in problem solving. Remember that you are not just looking for a solution, but one that will solve the problem to best meet your needs and objectives.
6. Always defer judgment when beginning to work on any problem. If you have trouble doing this, rapidly write down some possible solutions and corresponding weaknesses of each. Then throw away the list and begin again by defining the problem. Look for the middle ground rather than an easy solution.
7. After a period of intense concentration, take time to allow the problem to incubate.
8. Always ask "What's good about it?" whenever you or someone else suggests an idea. Never reject an idea outright.

Intellectual/Expressive Obstacles

1. Analyze the problem to determine the most appropriate language to use in solving it (e.g., verbal, mathematical, visual, etc.).
2. Don't limit yourself to just one problem-solving strategy; try using several different approaches.

3. Continually collect information about the problem throughout the process; ascertain the validity of all information obtained and separate facts from opinions.

Cultural Obstacles

1. Before rejecting a possible solution, consider if the reason for its rejection is due to some cultural taboo or to its lack of merit. Try to be aware of all taboos that may restrict your view of a problem.
2. Don't be afraid to break away from some traditions if the risks are relatively low and the outcome is likely to lead to a solution to an important problem.
3. Ask as many questions as you can think of about the problem; never be afraid to ask "why?" or "why not?"
4. When working on a problem in a group, be aware of any undue emphasis on competition or cooperation. Beyond maintaining minimal harmony in interpersonal relations, help insure that the group retains a problem orientation.
5. Don't be afraid to jump to conclusions after the problem has been defined. Explore all solutions based on intuition and feeling.
6. Allow yourself the freedom to fantasize and daydream about the problem, then try to relate these activities to achieving a feasible problem solution.
7. Look at what's humorous about your problem; use the problem's humorous aspects to suggest possible solutions.

Environmental Obstacles

1. Use problem-solving procedures to develop ways of gaining more time to work on your problems.
2. Actively solicit support for your problem-solving efforts by showing others how they might benefit from the solution.

3. Use distractions to suggest possible solutions; when the benefit from distractions has been gained, search for ways of eliminating, reducing, or accepting the distractions.
4. Learn to live with autocratic bosses, change their behavior, or leave the situation. Evaluate the negative consequences of each possible action.
5. Avoid overdependence on experts. Ask for information on the rationale or knowledge base underlying an opinion; seek to understand "why"; don't be afraid to seek second opinions.

Perhaps the most important requirement for overcoming creative-thinking obstacles is development of the proper mental attitudes. You first must learn to think positively about the obstacles. Most of them can be overcome or lessened in their effects if you believe they can. Second, you must be committed to overcoming the obstacles. Simply reading about the obstacles and ways of overcoming them will not be enough. You constantly must practice eliminating the obstacles and learn how to experience the sensations involved once you have overcome them. That is, you must be aware of when and to what extent you have mastered an obstacle. Finally, you will have to realize that much patience is required. Most of the thinking obstacles facing us took a long time to develop and emerge. Breaking down most of these obstacles also will take a long time to accomplish. Problem solving demands a great deal of perseverance, and so does creating the internal and external climates needed to become more effective creative problem solvers. More will be said on these matters in the next chapter.

3

DEVELOPING YOUR TRAINING PROGRAM

It's not easy to train for anything. Whether training for a career, job skills, an athletic event, or personal growth and development, considerable investments of your time, energy, and other personal resources will be required. In addition, if you really want to succeed at your training, you must be committed to achieving your objectives and persevere in trying to reach them.

There are no easy shortcuts available for any kind of personal change. This is why your personal expectations for training your creative mind are so important. If you expect to become more creative just by reading this book, you probably will be very disappointed. Developing a new way of thinking and solving problems is not something you can acquire through osmosis. You, instead, must become an active participant in your own development.

Part of your success in becoming a more creative thinker will be determined by the approach you use to train your creative mind. If you use a haphazard approach, the outcome is likely to be a diffuse mess of unconnected learnings and experiences. On the other hand, an overly structured approach is not likely to give you the flexibility needed to break away from conventional thought patterns. What seems to be required is a middle-ground approach— one that has some reason and order to it, but is not so confining as to inhibit creative insights and abilities.

The program outlined in this chapter is systematic without being excessively ordered. The exercises used to help train your creative mind have been presented in such a way to provide a gradual introduction to creative thinking. You should get all you can from one exercise before moving on to another. You always can come back if you don't feel you have completed one exercise to the best of your ability. Thus, it is not necessary that you rigidly follow any specific sequence; nevertheless, you should try to progress gradually through your program rather than skipping over those exercises that may look silly or too easy for you. No matter how well-developed your right brain is, a little practice always can be beneficial if you approach it with an attitude of learning something new.

The suggested program sequence is divided into three phases: 1) warm-up, 2) intermediate, and 3) applied. The warm-up phase consists of exercises that can be done with relatively little effort and without unduly "stretching" your right brain; the intermediate phase requires a greater amount of right-brain functioning; the applied phase is where you try to apply what you have learned to a sample problem and a personal problem. All three phases can be completed in about fifteen weeks, but you should try to continue with the program much longer. Many of the exercises can be repeated with additional benefit, and you can continue working on various problems in your life.

Before describing the program in greater detail, there are some aspects of your training that first need to be discussed. In general, these aspects concern the types of attitudes, awareness levels, and personal assessments that you must make to develop the climate within yourself needed for success in training your right brain.

DEVELOP THE PROPER MENTAL ATTITUDE

One of the first considerations you must deal with is your general attitude toward becoming more creative. Specifically, you must develop within yourself the belief that you will become creative. The more you expect to become more creative, the more likely it is that you will. This is known as a self-fulfilling prophecy.

One way you can begin to develop your own self-fulfilling prophecy is to recall the statement made in Chapter 1 about how we all are creative, but vary in the degree to which we have maximized our potential. If you buy this notion, then all you have to do is think in terms of becoming *more* creative, since you already are creative now. You've done it in the past, in spite of many obstacles, and there is no reason why you can't continue to develop in this direction. Think positively and you can become what you want to become. However, you must begin thinking this way today. Don't put off something as important as your own development.

LEARN TO RELAX

A second aspect of your program concerns your physical and mental awareness levels. Even with the proper mental attitude, your mind and body must be receptive to change and learning in a right-brain mode. Perhaps the best way to achieve this receptivity is through relaxation exercises. Such exercises can help rid you, at least temporarily, of various stressors that can inhibit your creative-thinking potential. Although you always should try to induce relaxation in yourself before beginning any of the creative-training exercises, your overall receptivity to the exercises will be greater if you practice relaxation techniques on a fairly regular basis.

One elementary relaxation procedure you can use is to focus on your breathing. First, lie down on the floor on your back or sit in a comfortable chair. Close your eyes and visualize all the tension flowing out of you. Feel it flow from your feet, your legs, your stomach, chest, neck, and shoulders. Allow several minutes for the tension to flow out. Then inhale deeply and hold your breath for about five or ten seconds, exhaling vigorously. Continue inhaling and exhaling in this manner for at least five minutes. While you are doing this, focus on the tension that is released each time you exhale. You should become progressively more relaxed each time you expel air. If you don't notice any change, then you need to concentrate more or eliminate some distraction in your environment.

You also can try any of the more elaborate relaxation methods. One such method is described next.

Begin by lying down on the floor or a hard bed with your legs uncrossed and your arms at your side. Clench your right fist with ever-increasing tension, being aware of how the tension affects your fist, hand, and forearm. Relax your fist and feel the tension ebb away. Do the same procedure again and then repeat it twice with your left fist. Then do the procedure simultaneously with both fists.

Next, bend your arms at the elbow and make your biceps as tense as possible. Try to be aware of how tense they have become. Release the tension and straighten your arms, feeling the relaxing sensations. Repeat this procedure at least one more time.

Move to your head, wrinkling your forehead as tightly as possible. Relax your forehead and visualize it becoming smooth again. Frown and then relax. Close your eyes and hold them closed very tightly, feeling the tension. Relax the tension around your eyes but allow them to remain closed for a few moments. Now, tense your jaw, biting down very hard. Relax your jaw. Press your tongue against the roof of your mouth as hard as you can. Allow your tongue to relax. Feel the absence of tension in your forehead, scalp, eyes, jaw, and tongue.

Tilt your head back and experience the tension in your neck. Roll your head to the right and left, noticing how the tension areas change. Relax and press your chin to your chest, feeling the tension in your throat and on the back of your neck. Return your head to a comfortable position and release the tension. Feel the muscles in your neck letting go. Now bend your head forward slightly and bunch up your shoulders, feeling the tension in them build. Relax your shoulders and sense the release spreading through your neck, throat, and shoulders. You should be feeling more and more relaxed now.

Tense your thighs and buttocks. Relax and try to notice the difference between the states of tension and relaxation. Tense your calves by bending your toes downward. Feel the tension. Now relax. Tighten your shins by curling your toes toward your face. Relax.

Finally, experience the sense of deep relaxation throughout the lower half of your body. Feel your feet, ankles, calves, shins, knees, thighs, and buttocks becoming more and more relaxed. Concentrate on these sensations for a few moments. Then imagine how this relaxed state is spreading up your body, to your stomach, lower back, and chest. Let more and more of the tension flow away. Feel the relaxation spreading to your arms, hands, and shoulders. Become more and more relaxed. Be aware of how loose and supple all your neck, jaw, and facial muscles have become.

You probably will get more out of this experience if you have someone read the instructions to you or if you record them for playback to yourself. If you do tape-record the instructions, be sure to allow sufficient pauses to experience the tension and relaxation activities.

ASSESS YOUR CREATIVE-THINKING CAPABILITIES

The third preplanning factor concerns the need for you to be aware of how creative you are and how much more creative you would like to be. Assuming that you do want to become more creative, there is no way you can evaluate a change in yourself unless you make some attempt to identify your current level of creative functioning. You have to know where you are before you can move ahead with any reasonable expectation of success. Then, once you have made an attempt to change yourself, you will be in a much better position to evaluate your effectiveness in training your creative mind.

Numerous instruments exist for evaluating creative abilities, and you might be wise to consult one or more of these in making a personal assessment. For example, there are the Torrance Tests of Creative Thinking (Torrance, 1974), Raudsepp's (1980) How Creative Are You? instrument, and Hermann's (1980) Learning Profile Survey Form (a measure of right- and left-brain dominance). Any one of these will provide you with at least a rough indication of your creative-functioning skills.

One relatively simple rating instrument of your creative problem-solving abilities is shown in Figure 3.1. It is geared specifically to the different types of exercises found in this book. However, it has no known scientific validity. In fact, it may mislead you as to your current creative problem-solving capabilities. And, because it is a self-assessment inventory, it would be difficult to tell if you actually do or do not act in the different ways described. Independent observations would be needed to make such determinations. Nevertheless, it could be helpful in forcing you to begin considering some of the major attributes involved in creative problem solving. At a minimal level, it may get you thinking more about the topic and help you in dealing with the final evaluation of your training program. Complete this instrument before beginning your program. Score yourself by simply adding up your numerical responses.

Figure 3.1 Creative Problem Solving Capability Rating Scale

Instructions: Using the scale that follows, rate yourself on each item according to how capable you believe you are in performing the activity described. When rating yourself on the items, try to think in terms of most problems you have dealt with rather than any particular problem. There are no right or wrong answers and your first reaction is likely to be the best.

1 = Not very capable
2 = Below average
3 = Average
4 = Above average
5 = Exceptionally capable

How capable do you consider yourself to be when it comes to:

1. Analyzing problem situations? _____
2. Being aware of and sensitive to different problem elements? _____
3. Being aware of problem constraints? _____
4. Testing major problem assumptions? _____
5. Using your different senses to help analyze the problem or generate ideas? _____
6. Rapidly generating ideas? _____
7. Deferring judgment when generating ideas? _____
8. Viewing a problem from many different perspectives? _____
9. Making remote associations among problem elements? _____
10. Forcing together two or more ideas or objects to produce something new? _____
11. Seeing something positive in every idea? _____
12. Evaluating and selecting ideas? _____
13. Anticipating possible solution consequences? _____
14. Tolerating ambiguity? _____
15. Gaining acceptance for your ideas? _____

DETERMINE YOUR CREATIVE READINESS

The final factor to consider before beginning your program is your creativity readiness. Readiness, in this regard, refers to how prepared and motivated you are to undertake the training program. Put another way, it is the extent to which you are predisposed to unleash your creative potential.

Being a capable creative problem solver is not all that is needed to develop your right brain fully. You also must possess the minimal resources and motivation needed to bring about a change within yourself. For example, unless you have the time required to devote to training your creative mind, it is not likely that you will achieve very much.

Examples of other types of readiness factors can be found in the Creative Thinking Training Readiness Scale shown in Figure 3.2. Complete this scale now. After you have rated each factor, add up the scores to find your total readiness index. If you scored between 40 and 50, you probably are ready to begin. A score between 15 and 39 suggests that you might want to reexamine some of the readiness factors with a low score to see what you might be able to change. It may be, for example, that some of the items you rated low would not be significant deterrents to you personally. Use your intuition. However, if you scored 14 or below, then you might want to rethink beginning the program. With such a score, your efforts are likely to be haphazard and you probably can't expect to gain much from them. However, it may be that you'll change your mind after beginning or that external conditions may change to justify starting the program. Thus, you should consider whether it would be best for you not to begin, to begin and see what happens, or to wait a few weeks or months to give it a try.

Figure 3.2 Creative Thinking Training Readiness Scale

Instructions. Using the following scale, indicate the extent to which each item is a concern to you in regard to your readiness for a creative thinking training program. For example, if you believe that you have plenty of time to devote to such a program, you might give that item a score of "5."

    1 = Critical concern
    2 = Important concern
    3 = Moderate concern
    4 = Mild concern
    5 = No concern

1. Time availability _____
2. Commitment to becoming more creative _____
3. Your willingness to take risks _____
4. Support (if needed) available to complete the program _____
5. Your willingness to persevere _____
6. Environmental distractions _____
7. Your openness to new experiences _____
8. Your desire to improve yourself _____
9. The extent to which you have clearly defined your life goals and objectives _____
10. Your overall motivation level _____

DESIGN YOUR PROGRAM

As mentioned, there are three phases suggested for you to follow: 1) warm-up, 2) intermediate, and 3) applied. There are thirty-seven exercises in the warm-up phase and thirty-eight in the intermediate phase. The applied phase is where you try to apply your learnings to a hypothetical situation and then to a personal problem of your own choosing. The hypothetical problem and a sample response are described in Chapter 11. Once you have worked through this problem, you then should attempt the same procedure with a personal problem you would like to solve.

The exercises suggested for the warm-up phase and the approximate time required or allotted for each are shown in Figure 3.3. Note that the exercises have been divided into blocks, each requiring approximately seventy-five minutes of time. You should try to complete each block within one week; do them in the order presented. Note also that the blocks are numbered, beginning with the bottom row, just as you would start a foundation for a house. If you can, you should average at least ten to fifteen minutes per day for five days during each week.

If you find that this pace is too slow or fast for you, you should make any necessary adjustments. You should not, however, try to complete the program too slowly or too quickly. If you do too little (e.g., one exercise a week), you are not likely to benefit from any cumulative learnings that might occur; if you do too much (e.g., the entire phase within one or two weeks), you won't have a chance to benefit from any incubation that might help you better understand your experience.

The suggested format for the intermediate phase is shown in Figure 3.4. The thirty-eight exercises in this phase are organized into six blocks with the same average time requirements as for the warm-up phase. Like the warm-up phase, you should use your own discretion in varying from the suggested amount of time to spend on the exercises each week. In both phases, however, you should follow the sequence of exercises within the blocks.They have been organized to approximate progressively more refined right-brain skills or degrees of difficulty and complexity.

Since the applied phase is described in greater detail in Chapter 11, I will not discuss it further here, other than to note that you should allow about two weeks for the hypothetical problem and two weeks for your personal problem.

Figure 3.4 Suggested Intermediate Phase Exercises

IV	Time (in minutes)	V	Time (in minutes)	VI	Time (in minutes)
7.15 Spy Stories	15	9.04 Category Crunch	15	10.04 You Can Take This Job and…	45
8.07 Label It	10	9.05 Weigh-In	20	10.05 I Scream	20
8.08 Light Up Your Life	15	10.03 Consultant	45		
8.09 Word to Word	15				
8.10 Name That Exercise	20				

I	Time (in minutes)	II	Time (in minutes)	III	Time (in minutes)
4.04 Early Bird	10	5.09 Cube Imagery	10	7.08 Gar * bägé	15
4.05 Imagine That	5	5.10 Orange Elephant	5	7.09 Go to Class	10
4.06 Bunny Hop	5	6.10 Just Like That	10	7.10 Don't Forget	5
4.07 Problem Detective	5	6.11 SDRAWKCAB	5	7.11 Column Relatives	10
4.08 Quadruple D	10	6.12 Would You Believe?	10	7.12 Just Alike Only Different	10
4.09 Nitty Gritty	10	6.13 Fantasyland	10	7.13 It Came From Beneath the Blot	10
4.10 What Problem?	15	6.14 Silly Inventions	15	7.14 What's In a Name?	15
5.08 Goodness Sakes	15	6.15 Just Suppose	20		

Figure 3.3 Suggested Warm-Up Phase Exercises

I	Time (in minutes)	II	Time (in minutes)	III	Time (in minutes)	IV	Time (in minutes)	V	Time (in minutes)
4.01 Goal Visualization	10	5.05 Sensory Stretch	5	6.08 Take a Stand	5	7.07 Word Relatives	6	8.06 Grid Lock	15
4.02 How Much Are You Worth?	10	5.06 Be a Banana	5	6.09 Take It Off	5	8.01 Steaming Ideas	25	9.01 Values	10
4.03 Think About It	10	5.07 Mowing Along	5	7.01 Brain Gusher	20	8.02 Fill-Out	10	9.02 Wired Up	10
5.01 Your Room	12	6.01 Square Off	5	7.02 Prefix-It	4	8.03 Draw-A-Word	10	9.03 Light the Way	10
5.02 The Picnic	5	6.02 Don't Fence Me In	15	7.03 Letter Hunt	6	8.04 Picture That	20	10.01 Idea Garden	15
5.03 Touch It	5	6.03 Create a New Viewpoint	5	7.04 Underweight	3	8.05 Something New	10	10.02 Freeze-Unfreeze	15
5.04 I Hear Ya	20	6.04 Switch Around	2	7.05 Word Chains	12				
		6.05 Symbol Relatives	10	7.06 Sniff Out	20				
		6.06 Spy Telegrams	5						
		6.07 Breakdown	20						

Before you begin your program, here are some tips you might want to consider:

1. Set aside a specific time each day to work on the exercises. If you can't set aside a specific time, you may need to do some of the exercises in your spare moments while commuting, waiting in airports, etc. If you do use such locations, carefully choose which execises you use, since many require rather intense periods of concentration.

2. Eliminate as many distractions as possible from your environment.

3. Always try to maintain the progressive aspect of the exercises. Don't skip around too much or you might lose some of the intended benefits.

4. If you don't complete an exercise within the prescribed time period, leave it and go on to the next exercise or do something else. Then return to it and try again. If you still can't complete the exercise, wait until you have finished the phase you are in or until you have finished one run through the program.

5. Try doing the program with one or more other people. There are several ways you might do this: You and one or more others could go through the program individually, then together; you could start the program as a group; or you could use two or more groups and develop a competitive spirit (not too competitive, however, since you don't want to create any unnecessary obstacles). If you do plan on using competition, it might be best if everyone completes the program alone first, or at least the exercises you plan to use during the competition.

EVALUATING AND MAINTAINING TRAINING PERFORMANCE

After you have gone through the entire program, you should spent some time assessing what you have learned and how you might have changed since you began. Such self-evaluations are not easy to do, since it often is difficult to be objective about your own performance. Nevertheless, you shouldn't consider your program complete until you have attempted some evaluation of your progress.

The most logical place to begin this evaluation would be with your personal goals and objectives. One way to do this would be to complete the Creative Problem-Solving Capability Rating Scale again (Figure 3.1). Do this without looking at your original responses. Then compare your two sets of responses and try to determine why you did or did not change in the direction you wanted. Next, determine in which specific areas you may need more practice. Finally, develop a plan to move yourself in the direction you want to go. For example, from your day-to-day experiences with the problems you encounter, you may decide that you still don't devote enough time to analyzing a problem. Think of how you might do this better and why you haven't been doing it. You might even repeat the exercises that deal specifically with the areas in which you still are having trouble.

Maintaining training performance is mostly a matter of being consciously aware of what thinking modes you need to use in dealing with different problems. If you recall, there are times in which logical, analytical, and verbal types of thinking will be best—analyzing a problem, organizing idea-selection criteria, and so forth. In contrast, right-brain, holistic, intuitive, and visual types of thinking will be best when your problem requires new perspectives, provides few solution guidelines, and involves rapid generation of large numbers of ideas, just to name a few characteristics. Again, both types of thinking are required to solve many problems, and the particular mode used often will vary with regard to the problem-solving stage involved. You must constantly be aware of when you should shift from one mode to another. If you lose this awareness, then you will be much more likely to revert to dominance by the left brain.

One way to help maintain this awareness is through

the use of refresher exercises. These exercises can come from any source as long as they involve right-brain thinking. I have selected twenty-eight exercises from this book that you could use for continuing practice. The numbers of these exercises are presented in Figure 3.5. Start with three to five exercises at a time, and continue to use them as long as you feel the need. Try to do these fairly rapidly and with as little effort as possible. Since you already will have been exposed to them, you also should try to stretch your right brain as much as possible in working through them. Don't view these exercises as simply repetitive, but rather as new opportunities to grow creatively.

Figure 3.5 Refresher Exercises

4.0l	6.13
4.02	6.14
4.03	
4.05	7.05
4.10	7.08
	7.11
5.01	7.12
5.02	
5.04	8.01
5.05	8.06
5.06	8.07
5.09	
5.10	9.02
	9.05
6.10	
6.11	10.01
	10.02
	10.03

GETTING READY

Before beginning work on a task, you need to gather the necessary tools. The nature of the task doesn't matter. Whether you are planning to write a book, fill out your income tax forms, plant a garden, or go to war, you have to be prepared to do the job. Painting a house, for example, involves deciding what to paint; assessing your ability and motivation to paint it; selecting a color or colors; choosing brushes, paint, and other equipment; and finally, preparing the surface to be painted (if necessary). Most or all of these activities must occur before any painting can begin.

The task of creative problem solving is no different. Before you can solve a problem creatively, you must be prepared. However, in contrast to most other tasks, there is little guarantee that creative methods always will resolve the problem. For this reason, preparation is critical for solving most problems requiring creative approaches.

Perhaps the most critical aspect of preparation is

self-awareness. Using an analogy from the house-painting example, the surface of the mind must be prepared properly before any problem solving can begin. However, the task now is more difficult since no simple tools exist for scraping away the old paint that has collected on your mind. As a result, you have to spend more time in analyzing the surface you want to paint creatively.

Analyzing your creativity surface should lead to greater awareness about your creativity potential. You must learn to tune in to the texture and other characteristics of the surface you'll be trying to change. You must learn, for example, in which spots the old paint is too thick and in which spots it is flaking off; where a wire brush is required and where sandpaper might be better. In other words, you need to learn those things about yourself that you can use to your best advantage when solving problems.

Another major aspect of preparation in creative problem solving is getting to know your problem. You must develop an awareness of what kind of problem you are dealing with, how it is put together, what is relevant and what is not, and how you must organize and process information about it to come up with a solution.

These two factors—self-awareness and problem awareness—are key ingredients for success in creative problem solving. Both ingredients can be obtained through preparation. Self-awareness must be prepared first, for without it you won't be able to develop many unique solutions. However, once you have self-awareness, most problems you encounter will be easier to solve. Problem awareness, in contrast, must be developed every time you face a new problem. Each new problem must be approached as a unique situation that presents a challenge. And the only way you can prepare for this challenge is by getting to know your problem.

The ten exercises in this chapter have been designed to provide you with practice in preparation involving both self- and problem awareness. The first five exercises ask you to look inward at yourself, to analyze how you solved problems in the past, to consider your creativity potential, and to practice with some ideas and visualizations. The remaining exercises are more problem-oriented and focus on speculation, processing problem information, looking for relevant problem elements, and creating new problem perspectives. All ten exercises will help you get ready for the exercises in the next chapters as well as for many of the problems you may encounter in your daily life.

4.01   Goal Visualization

We often become blocked in problem solving because of the negative mental attitudes we develop when we fail to solve some important problems in our lives. While we cannot always be successful in solving every problem we would like, the proper mental attitude can play an important role in increasing the number of problems we can solve.

Before beginning this exercise, assume that nothing is impossible and that every problem, no matter how difficult, can be solved.

Think of a problem you successfully solved in the past. Can you remember how you felt when you solved it? Did you feel happy, relieved, excited? Concentrate on these emotions for a minute. Did things turn out the way you originally had pictured them? Why or why not? If it will help, write down some of these reasons.

Now try to imagine how things will be if you are able to solve a current problem. What will you be doing? How will you feel? How will others feel? What will be better or worse? What will be the same or different? While you're doing this, see if you can develop mental images for every detail of your solved problem, no matter how unimportant the details may seem now.

If it will help, you also might try imagining what the ideal solution would be like and how you would feel if you achieved it.

4.02   How Much Are You Worth?

Several years ago it was estimated that the chemical elements in the human body were worth about $1.98. Of course, at today's inflation rate you could buy a condo in Hawaii for what you could get by selling your body's chemicals.

There also is another aspect of human worth that we often take for granted: the value that we have of ourselves. We can't assign a dollar value to it, but we can estimate its value in helping us achieve our creative potential. For unless we can accurately assess our positive features, we will be crippled when it comes to recognizing the positive features of ideas. Perhaps more important, however, is the ability to avoid dwelling on our liabilities. If we concentrate almost exclusively on our liabilities, then we will establish an almost insurmountable block to achieving our creative potential. Obviously we must be aware of our liabilities, but not to the detriment of our more positive attributes.

See how aware you are of your positive characteristics by doing the following:

> List everything about yourself that you consider to be of positive worth. Then describe how these characteristics could help you to enhance your creativity potential.

For example, if one of your positive features is always beng on time for appointments, then you might list reliability as something that indicates how you will be consistent in your approach to solving problems.

4.03   Think About It

The fact that you are reading this book indicates that you have some interest in becoming more creative. You even may have given some thought to a particular area of your life that you would like to enhance the most through creativity. It is only human to try and satisfy such needs.

However, concentrating on only one aspect of your life may be less than desirable from the standpoint of developing a well-rounded creative personality. You will receive more synergistic benefits if you are able to enhance your creativity in all your major life areas.

To start you thinking about this notion, make a list of all the things you could do to become more creative in different areas of your life. For example, what could you do to be more creative:

1. on your job?
2. in your relationship with your spouse or a close friend?
3. with your children or the children of others?
4. in your hobbies?
5. in your favorite sport or recreational activity?

To make this task easier, try listing the different types of activities or interactions involved in each area before you generate your creative alternatives.

4.04 Early Bird

The brain is an extremely complex instrument, capable of performing many different activities. Most of these activities occur consciously as we attempt to learn something or solve problems. Other activities, in contrast, occur below our conscious level.

Because there are so many different levels of brain activity, there is considerable variability in how we go about solving problems. For example, when we are trying to solve a particular problem, ideas often come to us at the strangest times—in the shower or while watching TV, driving, or reading, to name just a few. It is thought that such ideas emerge due to the subconscious processes of incubation. That is, even though we may not be concentrating on the problem, our brain is. At other times, ideas come to us only while we are consciously thinking about the problem.

One way we might benefit from the brain's various activities is to capitalize on different intensities of brain-wave functioning. Depending on the time of day and our level of arousal, the brain produces waves that vary from very mild to very intense activity levels. When the brain is idling—during sleep, for instance—what are known as theta waves can be observed; when the brain is busy processing large amounts of data, beta waves are produced. If it can be assumed that different aspects of the problem-solving process are associated with different brain-wave patterns, then this knowledge conceivably could be applied to help us in our problem-solving tasks.

For instance, theta-wave activity would be ideal for divergent, nonjudgmental types of thinking. Because many analytical brain functions are repressed when theta waves are present, there should be fewer barriers and constraints to creative thinking. Thus, by turning off some of the censors normally needed for rational, analytical thinking, the brain makes it much easier to free associate and speculate.

The difficulty involved in applying this knowledge, however, is that it is not clearly known how we can alter our brain waves to produce the most appropriate pattern. One possible solution is to use biofeedback. The trouble with this approach is that considerable practice may be required, and we cannot always be certain how reliably we can perform this task. Furthermore, not everyone has access to the equipment needed to use biofeedback. There is, however, another alternative.

By knowing when the brain is "holding" in different wave patterns, we can harness this information and apply it to our benefit. Thus, if we need divergent thinking, we can try to do it when theta waves are most likely to occur. It is thought that these waves are present most often right before we fall asleep and just before or right after we wake up in the morning.

Here's an exercise you can use to try harnessing your theta-wave brain patterns. It is simple to do and probably will work best with a problem you currently are working on.

1. Set your alarm clock to wake you up in the morning about twenty to thirty minutes earlier than usual.

2. As soon as you can, sit down and begin free associating solutions to your problem.

3. Suspend all evaluation while you are doing this and continue writing down solutions until you have exhausted all possibilities.

4. Jot down how long you spent on this activity.

5. Do the same thing the next morning, but try to write for five minutes more than you did the previous day. If you begin to run out of ideas before the time limit is up, keep writing even if what you put down doesn't seem to be practical or make much sense.

6. Continue this exercise for at least a week. Then stop and see how much you have improved.

4.05 Imagine That

Some people are successful at solving their problems because of their ability to imagine themselves doing something and experiencing various sensations. Many athletes, for example, will first visualize the actions they will perform before actually doing them. Pole vaulters often picture themselves running toward the bar, planting the pole, lifting off, and clearing the bar.

Your ability to do the same thing will help you in dealing with many of your problems. To test your ability to develop images, try the following, using as much detail in your visualizations as possible.

1. Think of yourself walking up some stairs.

2. Imagine the pain associated with a slight pin prick in your fingertip.
3. Feel a hot fire radiating off your back.
4. Visualize a rainy day in a forest.
5. Imagine the feeling of warmth when you first enter your house after being outside on a cold day.
6. Think of your bedroom when you were a child.
7. Imagine the sound of a jet airplane as it lands.
8. Picture yourself flying like a bird.
9. Imagine the feel and texture of a stucco wall.
10. Picture yourself riding a bicycle on a country road during the summer.
11. Picture yourself diving into a pool, at the moment you first hit the water.
12. Think of the smell of raw onions.

4.06   Bunny Hop

The development of creative solutions often involves the ability to rearrange information to form new meanings. See if you can make your ideas multiply like a bunny by forming as many words as possible from the word *rabbit*. Now try the word *multiply*. Think of at least twelve different words for each.

4.07   Problem Detective

When most of us first confront a problem, we often make snap judgments as to problem causes. A creative solution, however, is unlikely to be achieved unless we devote considerable time to analyzing the problem and generating a large number of possible explanations. In one sense, we must become "problem detectives" and try to guess what can be deduced from the problem situation. Because most unstructured problems provide few clues as to how they should be solved, we must initially develop many different hypotheses and then later test them for their validity.

Although the following statement is presented as a fact, it may or may not be true. Nevertheless, try to develop as many different explanations as you can.

Research has revealed that more people file for divorce during the summer than during any other season.

4.08   Quadruple D

Not all creative problem-solving activity involves creative, right-brain types of thinking. Throughout the problem-solving process, logical and analytical thinking also will be needed to process information used to achieve creative solutions. Furthermore, the large amount of information that often accompanies unstructured problem situations will require use of some type of systematic procedure to make sense of the information.

This exercise will provide you with the opportunity to practice your own analytical skills in systematically processing such information. Your task is to determine, from the information presented, who is the drunkard brother. You are to assume that being a drunkard is the drunkard brother's occupation and that each husband-and-wife pair lives together in the same city.

1. Four brothers lived in Detroit.
2. Dean married Dee Dee.
3. Dave moved to Denver.
4. The doctor brother moved to Duxbury.
5. Don married Darla.
6. Denise married the doctor brother.
7. The dentist brother married Danielle.
8. The druggist brother moved to Danville.
9. Dan married Denise.
10. Dee Dee lives in Dallas.

4.09   Nitty Gritty

The ability to separate the relevant from the irrelevant can be an important skill in problem solving. Making such distinctions, however, can be very difficult, especially when we are dealing with familiar things. Nevertheless, we must learn to see things in terms of their usefulness to us. Otherwise we would be overwhelmed by the amount of information we would have to process.

If you were to make improvements on the products that follow, which attributes would you consider to be relevant and which would you consider to be less relevant?
1. Roller skates
2. Telephone
3. Calculator
4. Stapler
5. Light bulb
6. Typewriter
7. Bicycle
8. Doorknob
9. Toaster
10. Clock

4.10   What Problem?

Perhaps the most frequent mistake made when trying to solve a problem creatively is plunging right in without considering the exact nature of the problem. Since a natural (or perhaps conditioned) tendency is to begin immediately generating solutions, any analysis of the problem frequently is skimmed over. Then, after making frustrated attempts to come up with workable solutions, it becomes apparent that the exact nature of the problem was never clearly defined. As a result, much effort and time are wasted that could have been applied more efficiently to defining the problem.

When initially stating a problem, it often is a statement that is either too broad or too narrow in scope. There are exceptions, of course, when we are able to formulate a problem statement that points us in the direction of a solution. The more common situation, however, is one in which the initial statement either constrains or clouds the direction we should take to work on a solution.

Whether or not this initial statement is too broad or too narrow is an individual matter. The perceived scope of the problem generally will vary from person to person. Nevertheless, there does need to be some awareness on the part of problem solvers as to how they tend to define problems. Thus, when you initially define a problem, you should constantly ask yourself if the problem is too broad or too narrow for *you* to deal with.

If you think a problem statement needs to be more broad or narrow, there is a way you can go about achieving the proper scope. In fact, you probably always should use this method regardless of how satisfied you are with your first definition of the problem. This method is simple, but very important in determining the eventual course of all your problem-solving efforts. Here's how it works: Simply ask Who? What? Where? When? Why? about the initial statement. Answer each question in as many ways as possible. Then, from among these answers, select the elements you would like to include in your refined problem statement.

To illustrate, consider the following problem:

In what ways can people be motivated:

Questions	*Possible Answers*
Who should be motivated?	Workers; students
What kind of motivation?	To achieve performance objectives; to do homework
Where is the motivation?	Within people; external to people; groups
When are people motivated?	When needs are likely to be satisfied
Why motivate people?	To get something accomplished; to satisfy needs

From these possible answers, the following refined problem statements could be formulated:

1. In what ways can students motivate themselves to do homework?
2. In what ways can worker needs be satisfied?
3. In what ways can workers be rewarded for satisfying their own and organizational needs?

Note that all these statements provide a focus different from the original statement, which was rather broad in scope. Also note that there is no such thing as a correct question or answer in using this method. The only objective is to create a new problem perspective that is either more narrow or broad in scope than the original.

This method also can be used to redefine problems that initially appear to be narrow in scope. For example, consider this statement:

In what ways can human hair be dried?

Questions	*Possible Answers*
Who needs their hair dried?	People
What kind of hair?	Human
Where is the hair?	On the head
When is the hair dried?	After it gets wet; when moisture is removed
Why dry hair?	So it won't be wet; to avoid catching cold

Possible restatements of this problem include:

1. In what ways can human head hair be dried?
2. In what ways can moisture be removed from human hair?

In contrast to the first problem, the analysis of the different answers revealed fewer and fewer and much less specific restatements. The analysis was not wasted, however, since the new perspective of removing moisture was gained. It is just such a perspective that could produce a creative solution to this problem.

Now try a similar analysis using these problem statements:

1. In what ways can interpersonal conflict be reduced?

2. In what ways can grass be cut?

COMMENTS AND SAMPLE ANSWERS

4.01   Goal Visualization

By first concentrating on the emotions you experienced after successfully solving a problem, you will begin to develop success assocciations that can help prepare you to deal with subsequent problems. However, be sure to pick a problem you recently dealt with to make it easier to recall your emotions.

Looking at the reasons you were able to solve this problem also will contribute to the development of these success associations. In addition, you may learn something that will help you the next time you face a similar problem.

When you practiced concentrating on your current problem, you should have imagined some of the same emotions you recalled from the previously solved problem. If you didn't have this experience, try to think of the reasons you didn't.

The most important aspect of this exercise, however, is to develop the creative climate within yourself that is so necessary for effective creative problem solving. For unless you have the proper mind set, you will be continually throwing up blocks to yourself. As the comic strip character Pogo said, "We have met the enemy and he is us." Creative problem solving is rife with constraints as it is. Try not to make yourself the major constraint.

4.02   How Much Are You Worth?

Positive Characteristic	*Contribution to Creativity*
1. I relate well to other people	Can help in gathering new sources of ideas
2. I can easily simplify complex ideas and concepts	Can help in finding the elegant yet simple solution and in clarifying complex problem situations

3. I am well-organized and efficient	Will help in putting together information in meaningful ways; will make it easier to see how things fit together to produce new ideas
4. I am tolerant of the beliefs and behaviors of other people.	Will make me more open to new ideas
5. I am a hard worker	Will provide me with the perseverance needed to solve many unstructured problems

4.03 Think About It

Whatever lists you developed for this exercise probably will be unique to you and others with similar occupations and interests. Thus, if your hobby is stamp collecting, you might think of different ways to obtain or display them. Someone whose hobby involves woodworking, in constrast, might think of ideas for new types of objects to make or ways to make them.

The important thing, however, is for you to think of as many different ways of doing things you do now—even if they are being done by someone else. If you do something differently than you have in the past, then you are expanding your own view of your activities and interactions. What other people do in these areas is not really important or relevant for this exercise. What you should hope to gain, then, is a greater awareness of how *you* are using your creativity in your different life areas and how this creativity could be enhanced.

4.04 Early Bird

What often happens when doing this exercise is that the initial solutions will be more logical and practical than those generated later in the week. Don't worry, however, since the ideas you produce in the middle or near the end frequently will result in the most creative solutions. They may appear to be illogical and impractical when you write them down, but if you spend a little time later in modifying them, you should be able to transform them into ideas with a high potential for solving your problem.

4.05   Imagine That

To receive the maximum benefit from this exercise, you will have to concentrate as much as possible on your visualizations. A quick thought and image of the different situations is not likely to provide you with much useful experience in visualization. You must really try to think very hard about each of the visualizations, imaging each activity in great detail. The more detail you are able to imagine, the more you will benefit.

If you didn't visualize many details, you probably were trying to do the exercise too quickly or you were just having trouble concentrating. In either case, you should try this exercise again when you can take your time and when you feel relatively relaxed. If they will help, you might even want to try a few deep-breathing exercises before beginning.

4.06   Bunny Hop

RABBIT		*MULTIPLY*	
bar	it	it	plum
bit	rib	ply	put
rat	bat	tulip	my
brat	bib	lip	mill
tab	bait	tip	pill
at	bra	pit	pull

4.07 Problem Detective

1. Most people take their vacations during the summer, are together more, and as a result, have more arguments.

2. Most people have wedding anniversaries during the summer and become depressed as another year of marriage goes by.

3. The heat makes people more irritable and leads to more arguments.

4. Children are out of school and family conflicts increase.

5. Extramarital affairs that are kept discreet during the rest of the year become known in the summer since people tend to be outdoors more.

4.08 Quadruple D

Although a few advanced thinkers might be able to solve this problem using unwritten mental gymnastics, it is actually quite easy for most of us to solve if we use a written, systematic procedure. All that is required is construction of a simple matrix using each of the four "D" categories of husbands, wives, cities, and husbands' occupations. Then it is just a matter of plugging in the information as it becomes available and returning to previous information when necessary to fill in the gaps. The answer, of course, is that Dean is the drunkard brother.

Husbands:	Dave	Dean	Don	Dan
Wives:	Danielle	Dee Dee	Darla	Denise
Cities:	Denver	Dallas	Danville	Duxbury
Occupations:	Dentist	Drunkard	Druggist	Doctor

Note that in contrast to the other exercises in this book, there is a correct answer to this exercise. This is essentially a very structured problem *if* you know the correct procedure to use in solving it. Otherwise you will see this problem as being very unstructured and be forced to use creativity to come up with some answer, although not necessarily the correct one as defined by the given constraints of the problem.

4.09 Nitty Gritty

What is relevant and irrelevant is pretty much a subjective matter. It all depends on your objective for the items listed. Thus, the color of a telephone will be irrelevant if your objective is to improve the telephone's functioning, but it will be very relevant if you are concerned with appearance.

Go back over the attributes you listed and think about why you categorized one attribute relevant and another irrelevant. See if you can learn anything about yourself in terms of the value preferences you have for products. For example, do you tend to value styling over reliability, or do you value both equally?

Another learning aspect of this exercise concerns the number of attributes you listed. How thorough were you when you listed the attributes for each product? Do you think that you listed every attribute that could be used to make an improvement? See if there are any attributes you left out. If you tried to visualize the products when doing this exercise you probably didn't list as many attributes as you might have had you looked directly at the product. However, it also may be that some of the attributes you left out were those that you consciously or unconsciously considered to be irrelevant. Again, your value judgments would come into play if this was the case.

4.10 What Problem?

1. Questions	Possible Answers
Who has conflict?	Blue-collar workers, husbands and wives
What kind of conflict?	Emotional, substantive

Where is the conflict?	On the job, at home
When is the conflict?	Working together; making a major purchase
Why is there conflict?	Differences in values and needs
or	
Why reduce conflict?	To achieve mutual objectives

Possible restatements:

   a. In what ways can interpersonal conflict among blue-collar workers be reduced?

   b. In what ways can persons who interact with one another better achieve their mutual objectives?

   c. In what ways can husband-and-wife differences in values and needs be reduced when considering a major purchase?

2. *Questions*	*Possible Answers*
Who has grass?	Homeowners
What kind of grass?	All kinds
Where is the grass?	In yards
When does the grass need cutting?	When it is over three inches in height
Why cut the grass?	To control weeds; for a nicer-looking yard

Possible restatements:

   a. In what ways can weeds be controlled?

   b. In what ways can grass be made to stop growing after it reaches a height of three inches?

WHAT'S HAPPENING

The ten exercises in this chapter are similar to the ones in Chapter 4, in that they will help you in developing self-awareness and problem awareness. However, most of the exercises in this chapter are designed to heighten specific sensory areas. There are exercises for your general powers of observation, hearing, visualizing, seeing, tasting, touching, smelling, and empathy. There also are exercises concerned with developing a positive mental attitude, concentration, and imagery.

If you make the most of these exercises, you should come away with an increased ability to learn from and experience your environment and the objects and people in it. For example, something as simple as an ashtray can be experienced in more ways than most people ever consider. Obviously, you can see an ashtray and touch an ashtray, but how often do you use your other senses to describe the same object? Have you ever considered tasting an ashtray? Somewhat repulsive, isn't it? Yet we do need to consider using all our senses to become better creative problem solvers.

It has been said that familiarity breeds contempt. It also could be said that familiarity breeds a dulling of our senses. Most of us become so immune to our daily environments that we rarely notice anything new or different unless it almost hits us in the face. The same often holds true for the problems we face. After a while we tend to view many problems as being similar or identical, when they may be very different variations of the same type of problem. Sometimes we have to fail to solve a problem to realize how much we took for granted about the problem.

If you want to avoid solving the wrong problem or failing to solve the right problem, then you will get a good start by charging up your sensory mechanisms. Unfortunately, many of us tend to rely on only one or two of our senses at a time and fail to appreciate all the other sensations available to us. The exercises in this chapter should help you realize that there is a whole new world out there waiting for you to experience. You just have to know what's happening.

5.01 Your Room

For this exercise, you will need to find a comfortable chair in a room of your choice.

The room you are in right now is "your room." Maybe it doesn't belong to you in the sense that you legally own it, but the fact that you are occupying space in it means that you have at least sensory ownership of the room. Therefore, begin to think of the room as *your* room and no one else's. You own it, and what happens in it is in your control.

Begin by describing your room. How large is it? Are there other people in it? If so, who are they and what are they doing? How many walls does your room have? What colors are they? What are they made of? What about the ceiling and floor? How are they different from the walls?

What objects are in your room? How are they arranged? Why are they there? Continue to visually explore your room in this manner for about five minutes, describing everything you can see. Then change your position and see if there is anything you missed. Can you see shadows now that you didn't see before? What about colors? Can you visualize how they might change during different times of day? Not including the number of objects, try to describe your room in at least thirty different ways.

Now go to another room and describe it in a similar manner. Only this time allow yourself only two minutes to describe as many different features as you can.

5.02 The Picnic

For this exercise, you first need to put yourself into a relatively relaxed state of mind. You will need to let your thoughts flow easily and to experience vicariously many different sensations.

Imagine that you are on a picnic in some secluded area far away from noises of the city. Your picnic site is an open, grassy area surrounded by trees, with a small stream nearby. You have brought a picnic basket and a blanket. You are there with a special friend and three children who are playing about thirty yards from you.

Begin by concentrating on this scene. Then try to gradually add more detail. What do the children look like? How are they dressed? What colors are they wearing? What are they playing? Where is the stream from where you are now sitting or standing? What does your picnic basket look like? How far away are the trees? Continue to add detail in this manner for another two or three minutes.

Now try to experience the many different textures present. What does the grass feel like? The blanket? The picnic basket? Can you imagine the textural contrasts of the different types of tree bark? Are there any rocks in your stream? If so, how do they differ in texture? Stick your bare feet in the stream. How does it feel?

Concentrate next on smells. Can you imagine what the grass smells like? What about the food in the picnic basket? What does it smell like? Does the blanket have a particular odor? Perhaps a horse just galloped through your picnic area and left its own special smell.

After you have thought of and attempted to experience all of the smells present, direct your attention to sounds. What do you hear? Listen very carefully. Can you hear yourself talking and the children playing at the same time? What does the stream sound like? Think of the wind blowing through the trees, and imagine the different sounds produced as the wind speed varies. Take an apple from your picnic basket and bite into it. What sound does it make? Think of other foods you might have in your basket and how they sound when eaten.

To receive the most benefit from this exercise, you will need to concentrate fully and attempt to introduce as much detail as possible.

5.03   Touch It

The sense of touch may be one of our less frequently used senses. We often take it for granted since we typically use some of our other senses more frequently. As a consequence, touching sensations will not be as well-developed as seeing, for example, due to limited sensory experiences in the touching area. In contrast, most blind people will exhibit greater facility in this sense than those of us who are "handicapped" by our seeing abilities.

In doing this exercise, try to shut out all your senses except touch. Ignore smells, sights, sounds, and tastes. Concentrate only on the sensations transmitted by your fingertips.

Place the following objects (or similar ones) in a medium-sized box or sack: a penny, a dime, a cotton ball, a pen or pencil, a small ball, a stick of gum, a key, a die or sugar cube, a small paper wad, and a square of sandpaper or an emery board. Without looking at any of the objects, reach in and identify each one by touch. Withdrawing your hand, try to visualize each object in as much detail as possible. Now reach into the box or bag again and examine each object by touch to see if you left out any features that you had visualized. For example, did you remember to visualize the raised portions on the coins and the rough edges on the dime? Did you have any trouble distinguishing the dime from the penny? Did the ball seem smaller or larger than you had imagined? Finally, select two objects at random (without looking) and compare them in as many ways as you can, using only your sense of touch.

5.04   I Hear Ya

Hearing is another sense that we frequently take for granted. Although we are exposed to a variety of sounds daily, we rarely hear them all. We are usually too busy thinking or attending to our other senses to hear everything going on around us. And with good reason, too. If we turned on all of our senses to their full capacity at the same time, we would be overwhelmed by the amount of data our brains would have to process.

To do this exercise, first imagine the following sounds:

the engine of a car or truck
wind blowing
bird calls
screeching tires
car horns
someone walking on a sidewalk
hands brushing clothing
people talking
dogs barking
sirens
your own breathing
music

Then take a walk on a relatively busy street and try to hear each one of these sounds, or any different ones. To do this, you will need to really concentrate, since what you are trying to do is *experience* the sounds and not just notice them.

5.05 Sensory Stretch

Although we are well equipped to experience our environment, the sensory mechanisms we use often deceive us. For example, if a person you know to be six feet tall stands a quarter of a mile from you, he or she will appear to be much shorter to the unaided eye. Obviously, the person's height doesn't change. What does change is our perception of the situation. In a similar manner, heat radiating from a highway on a hot day will look like water when viewed from a distance. Again, our perceptions are distorted by our sensory mechanisms.

When you think about it, we are constantly being misled by our senses. Perhaps what is needed is "truth in sensing" legislation. We could then mandate that whenever our senses distort reality, they would be penalized in some manner. That would certainly teach them.

Until such legislation is put into effect, perhaps the next best thing would be to become more aware of the limits of our senses. One way to do this is to exaggerate or stretch the functions normally performed by each of the five senses.

As a test of how in tune you are with your senses, answer the questions that follow. For each answer, try to think of why you responded the way you did.
1. What color is happiness?
2. What color is Monday?
3. What does blue smell like?
4. How would you describe the texture of yellow?
5. What does a peach sound like?
6. What does red taste like?
7. How would your eyes feel if they could "touch" sandpaper by only looking at it?
8. What does a ray of sun smell like?

9. What does a rose look like to another rose?
10. What color is the ticking of a clock?

5.06   Be a Banana

The ability to empathize with living and nonliving things is a critical skill required of all creative thinkers. Empathy helps create awareness that can lead to understanding. And understanding is essential for dealing with most kinds of problems. Without it, we can only bring limited resources to bear on our problems. In fact, creative solutions to some difficult problems can be achieved only by becoming deeply involved with the problem. Thus, we probably should try to become a problem whenever possible. In doing so, new insights will be revealed that could not be obtained from just being on the outside looking in.

Using all the concentration you can, try this exercise: You are a banana. You live in a rain forest in South America. It is raining, and tiny droplets are running off your skin. Feel the droplets. Let them soak the surface of your skin. Smell the rain. What does it smell like?/It now has stopped raining. A cool breeze is blowing, and you and the other bananas are bouncing around, swaying in the wind. Feel the wind and experience the motions. What sensations are there as your skin rubs against the skins of the other bananas? Look down and see the ground as you sway back and forth. Look up and see the tops of the trees./Now the wind is dying down. The oppressive heat is returning. Feel the warmth of the sun on your skin. Let the last bit of moisture on your skin dry up and evaporate./Suddenly there is tension in the air. Hear the birds in the trees around you call out their warning sounds. Feel the pressure on your tree. You are now swaying in jerky movements, but there is no breeze. The movements stop. An intense pressure grips you and squeezes ever tighter. Feel this pressure as you are being squeezed inward./Now you are being torn away from the other bananas by a large hairy hand. Feel the hand's texture on your skin. Hear the sound that is made as your stem is cracked and twisted./You are now separated and without the contact of the other banana skins. But the intense pressure continues. A sharp pain develops in the end of you. A small cut is made in one of the seams of your skin. Feel this pain and experience the small amount of air that enters the cut./Now your skin is being ripped down your side in large strips ... one, two, three, four strips. Your insides are now exposed and shocked as they try to adjust to the sudden lack of warmth and darkness. Feel the sun and air on your fruit. What does it smell like?/You are now completely free of your skin. Hot animal breath is enveloping you and it is becoming dark. Sharp incisors cut into your upper half, tearing it away from the lower. Imagine the fibers being torn away as your fruit is mixed with saliva. Feel the juice from your fruit and the saliva mixing together. Now your bottom half is gone. Don't you wish you were an animal?

5.07   Mowing Along

Write down three to five comments about the proposed design for a lawn mower shown in Figure. 5.1.

5.08   Goodness Sakes

Many potentially useful ideas are lost because of our inability to suspend judgment and look for the positive aspects of new ideas. While not all ideas are initially proposed in a workable form, a few changes often can lead to a much more feasible idea. In addition, what frequently appears to be a silly idea to one person will be used by another person as a stimulus for more practical solutions. In this respect, there is really no such thing as a silly idea, since all ideas have hidden within them the potential to produce the solutions we are looking for. It simply takes a little digging around to find these solutions.

See if you can think of at least three positive aspects for each of the following proposed products. If you can't think of anything positive, try to develop some modifications that might make the idea workable.

Figure 5.1 Proposed Design for a Lawn Mower

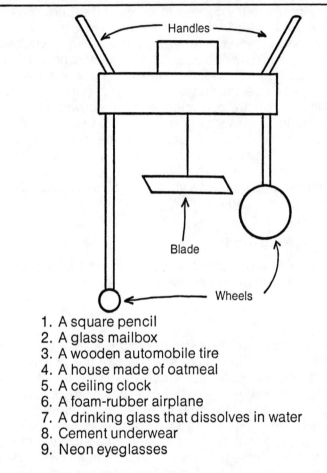

1. A square pencil
2. A glass mailbox
3. A wooden automobile tire
4. A house made of oatmeal
5. A ceiling clock
6. A foam-rubber airplane
7. A drinking glass that dissolves in water
8. Cement underwear
9. Neon eyeglasses

5.09   Cube Imagery

One important function served by the right brain is manipulation of spatial relationships. The ability to recall and visualize images occurring in space is as essential to creative thinking as is the ability to recall and use words. Unfortunately, not all people exercise their visualization skills as much as they could; consequently, they believe they are not very good at visualization. With a little practice and concentration, however, all of us can improve this important skill greatly.

Repeat this exercise several times until you can do it easily.

First, visualize a row of three cubes in front of you. The cube in the center is yellow and those on the ends are green. Now imagine that you move the yellow cube to the right end of the row and the cube on the right end to the center. What is the order of colors?

Easy? OK, then imagine that you move the cube now in the center to the left end and the cube that was on the left end to the right end. Now what does the row of colors look like?

No challenge? Well, make it more difficult by starting over again with two rows, the first with three green cubes and the second with three yellow cubes. Take the green cube on the left end and exchange it with the yellow cube in the middle. Then take the yellow cube on the right end of the second row and exchange it with the green cube in the middle of the first row. Finally, take the cube on the left end of the first row and exchange it with the cube in the middle of the second row. What is the order of colors in the two rows?

5.10   Orange Elephant

Get ready to time yourself. Do you have a watch or a clock with a second hand? Good. Now, for the next fifteen seconds, concentrate real hard on *not* thinking of an orange elephant. OK, time's up. Now tell the truth. Didn't you think of that elephant at least once during the fifteen seconds? It's not so easy to do, is it?

A simple act of concentration can be very difficult, depending on your state of mind, the external environment, and the amount of practice you've had in really concentrating on something. Yet, concentration is essential for creativity or any type of activity that requires focused effort.

We all differ in our ability to concentrate. Just think of the study habits you and your friends had while in school. Some people seem capable of intense study even under the most adverse conditions, including the sounds of blaring radios and TVs. Other people, in contrast, tend to be disturbed by the slightest sound.

One thing is fairly certain, however. Our concentration skills can be improved with practice. To see if you can improve your skills in this area, try this exercise.

Multiply 3×2 in your imagination. As you do it, think of each number and the final product. Do the same thing with 30×2, 30×3, and 40×6. Now multiply the following numbers and try to concentrate as hard as possible on all of the operations involved: 130×2, 130×3, 130×4, 24×2, 24×3, 24×4, 125×2, 135×3, and 145×4.

COMMENTS AND SAMPLE ANSWERS

5.01   Your Room

If you are basically an unobservant person, you might have had some trouble with this exercise. Even if you do consider yourself to be observant, however, you still might have had some difficulty in noticing and describing everything in your room.

The primary reason for this difficulty is that most of us are afflicted with a disease known as familiarity, which tends to breed a fixed way of thinking and seeing, and from which it is very hard to break away.

We often are the least observant about the environment we live in every day. Once we travel to a new environment, however, everything changes. We are suddenly bombarded with a wide array of stimuli that demand our immediate attention. We even can have trouble taking in everything and assimilating it so as to provide us with meaning. This is not the case in our own backyard, where the environmental stimuli have long since ceased to evoke much of a reaction from us.

Try to rev up your right brain a little each day by noticing something new in your everyday environment. Maybe it will be as simple as noticing the texture of the roof on the house across the street from yours. It really doesn't matter what you notice or how you do it. All you need is to awaken those stimuli that died so long ago. If you can do this on a regular basis, then you will do something positive to make your right brain a little more alive every day.

5.02   The Picnic

If you had trouble with this exercise, it may have been caused by trying to rush through it too quickly. To experience all the sensations, you need to allow sufficient time for the appropriate connections to be made within your brain. An imagery exercise such as this requires more time than direct experiencing of sensations. If you think you missed out on all the experiences available, try the exercise again.

The ability to perform this type of exercise is critical to development of sensory awareness about all types of problems. For without this awareness, we can overlook problem characteristics that could be vital to achieving a creative solution.

5.03   Touch It

You should have experienced little difficulty in identifying the different objects by touch. The only exception might have been the difference between the penny and the dime, since they are similar in shape and size. You were forced to rely almost exclusively on touch to make this distinction.

Visualizing the objects and then attempting to identify them by touch often can produce surprising results. Even though we are familiar with these objects through both senses of sight and touch, the seeing sense will predominate due to its ability to provide more of the information needed to use the objects. Thus, if I decide to use my pen, I only need to look at it, recognize its general shape and size as a pen, and put it to use. Although I can do the same thing with only my sense of touch, it will take a little longer to make the connection than using recognition by sight. In this case, I must first recognize the texture, material, and shape of the pen, and then determine which end the cap is on so I can remove it and begin writing. With the sense of sight, these operations are performed almost simultaneously.

You should have experienced similar differences with the other objects. If not, repeat the exercise and concentrate more on the differences between these two senses.

The comparisons you could have made between any two objects probably involved comparisons of size, shape, and texture. For example, the key and the small ball could have been compared by noting how the ball is round in shape, smaller in length, but broader than the key; and that the ball is smooth in texture on all surfaces, as is the key, but that the key has an irregular shape.

5.04 I Hear Ya

How successful do you think you were in hearing the sounds? Obviously, unless you have a deafness problem, you can hear the sounds. But can you *experience* them as separate sounds of environmental stimuli? What about sounds that occur at the same time? Can you easily distinguish between two or more sounds?

You also should try to pay particular attention to the various characteristics of the different sounds. Are you able, for example, to detect easily differences in pitch, timbre, and amplitude? Notice also any contrasts between these characteristics of the different sounds. From a qualitative standpoint, are you able to sense the upper ranges of sounds such as bird calls and screeching tires? How are they different? Continue to examine these sounds in as many ways as you can, until you believe that you have begun to master them.

5.05 Sensory Stretch

What you should hope to gain from this exercise is a feeling for how easily you can distort your sensory mechanisms and apply them to other functions. While there can be no right or wrong answers, you may find that you are able to shift some sensory functions more easily than others. For example, it may be that you can quickly think of the color of an intangible feeling, but have some difficulty experiencing the smell of a color.

The reasons you gave for your answers may be a clue to your experiential background. Thus, if you described Monday as blue, it may be due to a depressed feeling you have on Mondays, or simply that you have picked up on the general notion of "blue Mondays." In a similar manner, if you described the texture of yellow as smooth, you may be reacting to a colored substance you use every day, such as butter.

If you did have trouble in distorting any of your senses, try to think of any possible reasons. Such trouble may stem from certain deficiencies in your sensory background experiences. People with their full eyesight, for example, often have a less highly developed sense of hearing than blind people. Although such a difference may not really be thought of as a deficiency by many sighted people, it does dramatize how we don't always fully develop the potential of our senses. Ultimately, heightened sensory awareness will go a long way toward making us more creative.

5.06 Be a Banana

Some people have trouble doing this exercise because they really don't concentrate on all of the sensations involved. To benefit from this experience, you have to intensely focus your senses so that you can achieve a maximum level of sensory arousal. Another problem people have is that it is difficult to experience the sensations when you have to transfer the information from your eyes to your brain. You will find that it is much easier to do this exercise if you have someone read it to you while you close your eyes, relax, and try to concentrate.

5.07 Mowing Along

If you made any of the following comments or similar ones, try this exercise again:
1. It is too high off the ground.
2. One of the wheels is too big (or too small).
3. It has two handles, where only one is needed.
4. The handles are too short.

Note that all of these comments have negative connotations. Although such criticism is not entirely undesirable, too much can easily stifle creativity. Unfortunately, most of us have been conditioned to respond in an almost entirely negative manner. So try again, only this time see if you can notice the positive aspects. For example, the blade could be made retractable, so when it encounters large objects it moves out of the way; the two handles make it easy to push the mower from either direction; the size difference in the wheels would make the mower ideal for mowing down steep hills.

5.08   Goodness Sakes

1. Won't roll off tables.
   Easy to store in square containers.
   Will clamp more securely in a modified drawing compass.
2. Easy to see when the mail has arrived.
   Could double as a miniature greenhouse for plants.
   Could be used to trip a solar cell when mail is placed inside and signal that the mail has arrived.
3. Eliminates flats.
   Low cost.
   Could be burned when worn out.
4. Easy to build or remodel—just heat and add water.
   Fire-resistant.
   Good insulator.
   Could eat for breakfast; available food for emergencies.
   Might be easy to sell to a Quaker (sorry about that!).
5. Easy to locate.
   Would strengthen neck muscles.
   Could double as a light fixture.
   Could be connected to a long, vertical rod that would rotate plants in accordance with the outside light.

6. Crash-resistant.
   Would float if crashed in water.
   Could recycle as pillows.
   Passenger legs could be stretched more inside.
7. Perfect for people who belong to "Waterholics Anonymous."
   Would require no washing.
   Ideal for bars who want to sell alcohol-only drinks.
8. Would help in losing weight through perspiration.
   Could use as a weight for scuba diving.
   Could use for athletic conditioning.
   Would provide protection from groin injuries.
9. Could sell all of them to Elton John.
   Could use to see in the dark.
   Could use as emergency flashers.
   Would provide an ideal advertising medium.
   With the right type of light, would help repel bugs.
   Could modify and use for a facial suntan.

5.09   *Cube Imagery*

If you could do this last set of operations easily, then you already have pretty good visualization skills. Perhaps what you have learned to do is memorize the sequence of colors after each operation and then make the necessary adjustments. This is the way most people will perform this exercise.

If you had trouble visualizing the different moves involved, try reading one of the moves, then shut your eyes, fixing it in your memory. Concentrate on the pattern until it becomes locked in. Then do the same thing until all the moves are completed and you can see the final pattern of colors. If you still are having trouble, it may be that you are not able to concentrate now and need to try some other time. Also, if you try to hurry through this exercise, it will be much more difficult to do. Most of us aren't used to performing mental manipulations of this nature, and time is required to practice the different stages involved.

5.10   Orange Elephant

If you had trouble performing any of the calculations, try thinking of that orange elephant. First, fix the numbers firmly in your mind. Then, each time you come up with a digit in the total, think "orange elephant." This way, you should be able to recall the total much easier. For example, to multiply 125×2, think $5 \times 2 = 10$, zero orange elephant. Carry the one and $2 \times 2 = 4 + 1 = 5$ orange elephant and then $2 \times 1 = 2$ orange elephant. Put together the orange elephants and you have the total, 250.

If you had trouble fixing the numbers in your imagination, you also can use the orange elephant to help. One way to do this is to think of the numbers as large numerals in a vivid orange color. State each number and say "orange elephant." Then proceed with the calculations. Thus, to fix 145×3, you would visualize the 1, 4, and 5 and say "145 orange elephant times 3 [visualized] orange elephant." If this doesn't work for you, assign a different color to the number in the second row—say, blue. Then you would proceed by saying "145 orange elephant times 3 blue elephant."

Keep practicing with the exercise until you can perform all of the operations with ease. If you feel you have mastered this exercise using the numbers involved, select your own numbers to use. Or, if you would like a slightly different challenge, try using division problems.

6

LOOSENING UP YOUR MIND

Most forms of left-brain, analytical problem solving involve the logical and systematic application of old ways of looking at problems. When using this method, problems first are diagnosed and then a known solution is used to produce the desired result. The outcome of this approach will be either a correct or incorrect solution. Right-brain, creative problem solving, in contrast, involves developing new ways of looking at problems without regard to any logical or systematic procedure. Furthermore, creative solutions can't be judged in terms of their correctness or incorrectness, since one approach is no more likely than another to produce a creative outcome.

Development of new ways of looking at problems

requires a considerable amount and variety of mental flexibility skills. If you can't judge a solution as to its correctness, then you must be able to produce many different ways of viewing the problem. In addition, you must be able to break away from any constraints you place on yourself that might decrease your flexibility. Finally, you must constantly test any and all assumptions you might make about a problem. If you lock in on one particular course of action or viewpoint, you won't be able to produce very many unique solutions.

All of the fifteen exercises in this chapter are intended to help you loosen up your creative mind. The major objective is for you to develop the ability to look at problems in new ways and with a fresh eye. Among the specific flexibility areas covered are: breaking away from constraints, testing assumptions and problem boundaries, categorizing and redefining symbols, breaking down and analyzing problems, analogies, reversals, distortions, fantasy, and hypothetical situations.

6.01   Square Off

Here's a classic exercise that is quite useful for helping us to remember the importance of not making unwarranted assumptions based on our initial perceptions.

How many squares are there in Figure 6.1?

Figure 6.1 Square Exercise

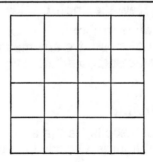

6.02   Don't Fence Me In

One of the most frequent constraints we place on ourselves as creative problem solvers is making unwarranted assumptions about the boundaries of the problem we are trying to solve. Such assumptions typically are reflected in our initial statement of the problem. When we blindly accept the limitations imposed by these statements, we are in danger of succumbing to unneeded conceptual rigidity. For example, the problem of increasing parking spaces on an overcrowded college campus contains the assumption that cars are the only means of transportation available. Why not use buses or trolley cars to carry students from remote parking lots? Another assumption would be that the on-campus parking spaces are the only ones available.

To help break away from this constraining tendency, identify the assumptions made in the following problem statements:

1. To design a battery-powered calculator capable of performing all the operations needed by an accountant.
2. To build a better garbage can.
3. To design a better door lock for the home in order to reduce burglaries.
4. To design a telephone cord that won't tangle and makes it easy to use the receiver from a distance of at least fifty feet.
5. To design scissors that are less fatiguing to use.

6.03   Create a New Viewpoint

Look at the drawing in Figure 6.2. Describe everything you see. Do the patterns have any meaning for you? You should be able to detect two different types of patterns. Do you see them?

6.04   Switch Around

Another aspect of flexibility is the ability to observe rapid changes in visual figures. Quickly look over the top three drawings in Figure 6.3. Then select the one drawing (A,B,C, or D) that comes next in the series.

Figure 6.2 What Do You See?

6.05   Symbol Relatives

The ability to classify symbols according to their similarities and differences can be extremely helpful in developing new problem perspectives and in breaking away from conventional problem constraints. Categorization of information into related or unrelated categories is essential for all of the stages of the creative problem-solving process. Thus, the more practice you have in this skill, the better equipped you will be to attack unstructured problem situations.

Try to break away from conventional thinking and list at least ten different ways that at least four groups of the symbols in Figure 6.4 are similar. For example, the symbols

Figure 6.3 Which Drawing Comes Next?

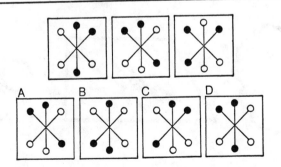

Figure 6.4 How Are the Symbols Similar?

numbered 1, 2, 5, 8, and 11 all contain or enclose other symbols.

6.06   Spy Telegrams

Haven't you always wondered how well-developed your symbolic redefinitional skills were? Haven't we all? Well, you can test them now with this exercise. Assume that you have intercepted ten telegrams from an enemy spy. Contained within each telegram are at least two secret code words formed from the letters of two or more consecutive words. For example, in the sentences, "TALKING IS TABOO. KEEP QUIET," one word is GIST and another is BOOK. The word KING, however, would not count, since it is not part of two or more consecutive words.

Locate at least two secret code words in each of the following ten telegrams:

1. SAW ARCHANGEL LEAVE TODAY.
2. CLIMB OR ROW QUICKLY.
3. FORGET BOMB AS TOO LATE.
4. WENT TO TIMBUKTU. LIP SORE.
5. LOST MY LIGHTER. UGANDA IS HOT.
6. TRUCK BROKE DOWN BUT TONNAGE STILL O.K.
7. PUT IT ON MY TAB. LEAVE THE RESTAURANT.
8. CANNOT FUFIL TERRIBLE EDICT.
9. SAW ONE ACRE. ATE A COW.
10. AM ON THE PAMPAS TO RALLY SUPPORT.

6.07   Breakdown

Creative problem solving usually involves restructuring problems so that new perspectives can be achieved. By creating a new way of looking at a problem, unique ways of dealing with it can be revealed. Thus, the better we are at breaking down problems and producing new perspectives, the more likely it is that we can come up with creative solutions. A one-sided view of problems, in contrast, generally will produce only mundane and conventional solutions.

This ability to pull apart problems requires some practice and a great deal of persistence. And the task is made all the more difficult by our self-imposed perceptual constraints. As Charles Kettering once noted, you can't see the view from the bottom of a rut. It is up to us to practice and persevere in climbing out of our ruts.

This exercise will help you to develop figural flexibility, perseverance, and the ability to identify and analyze relevant problem information. Look at Drawing A in Figure 6.5, and then note the different ways it has been broken down, as shown in Figure 6.6. These are only a sample of the many different ways this figure could have been broken down. You already may have noticed several other possible breakdowns. Now look at Drawings B and C in

Figure 6.5 Drawings for the Breakdown Exercise

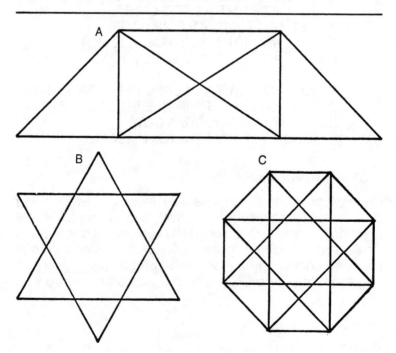

Figure 6.6 Some Possible Breakdowns of Drawing A

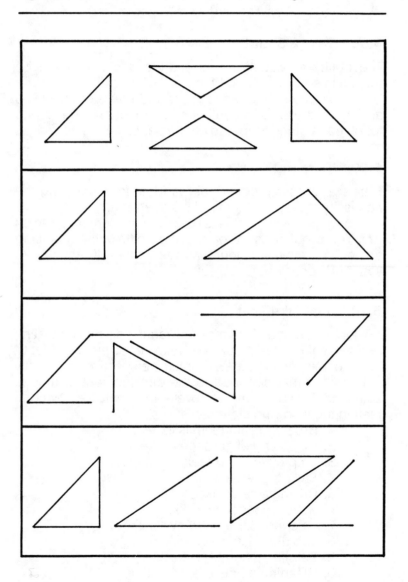

Figure 6.5 and try to draw four or five different breakdowns of each. Do more if you can.

6.08 Take a Stand

The ability to visualize and analyze a situation will be helpful in solving this problem.

Take a sheet of newspaper and figure out how you and one other person could stand on it but not be able to touch each other. Stepping off the paper is not allowed.

6.09 Take It Off

Here's a classic problem that is ideal for illustrating the necessity to view problems with a fresh eye.

An open wine bottle is placed in the center of a small rug. The problem is to remove the bottle without spilling any of its contents or touching the bottle with any part of your body or any other object.

6.10 Just Like That

Analogies are one of the most powerful tools for stimulating problem solutions. By looking for similarities among objects, ideas, or relationships, new problem perspectives frequently are created that can lead to the development of unique solutions. Try your hand at developing analogies by completing the following statements:

1. Brushing your teeth is like ...
2. Disposing of garbage is like ...
3. Employee absenteeism is like ...
4. Saving energy is like ...
5. Driving a car is like ...
6. School vandalism is like ...
7. Littering of the highways is like ...
8. Job dissatisfaction is like ...
9. Painting a house is like ...
10. Cleaning a house is like ...

6.11   SDRAWKCAB

One handy way to gain a new perspective on a problem is to reverse the initial problem statement and analyze it for any possible solutions. Thus, if you are interested in how to improve a car's gas mileage, think of how you might *decrease* it. A large deflector, for example, might be placed in front of the car, perpendicular to the ground, so that the car's movement would be slowed down, thus consuming more gas. Although such an action is not likely to solve the original problem, it could suggest a more plausible solution. By modifying the deflector to smooth the flow of air under the car, for instance, air resistance would be decreased and would result in increased gas mileage.

Before you practice this backward way of looking at problems, keep one thing in mind: It is not how you reverse the problem that is important. Rather, it is important to reverse the problem in as many ways as possible. There is no such thing as a correct problem reversal.

Reverse the following problem statements in as many ways as you can:

1. How to make meetings more efficient.
2. How to increase employee job satisfaction.
3. How to reduce street crime.
4. How to reduce or eliminate arson.
5. How to prevent football injuries.

6.12   Would You Believe?

The act of distorting a problem situation is another way to provide new problem perspectives and to develop unique solutions. Comedians, for example, rely heavily on distortion and exaggeration, since stretching the facts about a situation in an unusual or unexpected manner is the basis for many types of humor.

The same principle can also be applied to more concrete problem situations. By simply listing the desired objectives for a problem and then exaggerating each one, a new way of looking at the problem is created that often will lead to a creative solution. However, like other similar approaches, it is not the type of exaggeration that is important, but rather, the fact that any exaggeration or stretching of the problem is attempted.

To illustrate, a problem of how to develop a better briefcase might be set up as follows:

Original Objective	Exaggerated Objective	Possible Solution
Lightweight	No weight	Use no metal; use self-reinforcing, vinyl materials
Easy to open	Always open	Opens on touch; use outside pockets
Secure from unauthorized entry	Opens only for owner	Voice-actuated locks

Now here's a problem you can practice with: Develop a better copying machine.

6.13   Fantasyland

Another way to break away from the constraints we often impose on ourselves is to assume that anything is possible—that is, to assume that there are no constraints. Constraints do exist, of course, but unless the mind is given freedom to speculate, unique solutions will not have the opportunity to emerge.

To illustrate, a problem of how to prevent vandals from breaking windows in school buildings might be resolved by proposing that the windows disappear. Eliminating the windows or using break-resistant plastic panes instead of glass then might be used as more practical solutions.

Go on your own trip to fantasyland and try to develop fantasy solutions for the following problems (include, if you can, practical solutions):

1. How to reduce highway accidents.
2. How to eliminate typing errors.
3. How to prevent water damage to houses in flood-plain areas.
4. How to develop a carpet that never gets dirty.
5. How to prevent air loss in automobile tires.

6.14   Silly Inventions

Fantasy can be a valuable ally to the creative problem solver. Stretching the mind beyond what is usually considered to be rational often can lead to unique and productive thinking as well as highly creative solutions.

This exercise is designed to promote flexible thinking and to provide an opportunity to practice suspending judgment. It can be especially fun when done with a group of people who can make a game out of it by judging who thought of the silliest invention. Remember, today's silly invention might be tomorrow's hot product idea.

To do this exercise, think of the silliest idea you can for a new invention or modification of a present product. Describe in some detail what this invention will be capable of doing.

6.15   Just Suppose

We often become blocked in our thinking because of the difficulty we have in overcoming environmental constraints. If we could imagine a different environment, the constraints we normally face might be easier to overcome.

Just suppose that everyone was restricted to a wheelchair and had the use of only one finger on one arm. How would life be different under these circumstances? To exercise your creativity in responding to this question, design a house that will be suitable for such a person to live in. For example, what changes would have to be made in each room of a typical house? How would appliances have to be designed? If everyone had these constraints, what new entertainment activities might be developed? What new cooking utensils would be needed? How would doors be opened and closed? Would doors still be needed? Think of as many different innovations as you can for this house.

COMMENTS AND SAMPLE ANSWERS

6.01   *Square Off*

There are at least thirty-five squares. They can be found using the sixteen small individual squares, different positions of two-by-two and three-by-three squares, the four-by-four square that forms the border, and the five squares formed by using the individual squares themselves as borders. More creative viewpoints might yield even more squares.

If you are like many people, your initial response was sixteen and then perhaps seventeen squares if you included the border. You may never have considered combining the small squares to form larger ones. If you did fail to do this, then you were making an incorrect assumption about this problem. And the reason you made this incorrect assumption probably had to do with the constraints you placed on yourself. In this instance, you would have been constrained by thinking of a square as a unitary figure rather than one that can be put together with others to form additional squares.

Can you think of other times you might have placed similar constraints on yourself when trying to solve a problem? Most of us can easily recall such situations; it's really nothing to be ashamed of. However, if we are ever to overcome the constraints we place on ourselves, we must continually test all assumptions we make about all problems.

Incidentally, one assumption about this problem is that the squares are located in unidimensional space (i.e., a flat plane). What would happen if the problem was considered as existing in multidimensional space? If the problem was seen in more than one dimension, then the number of squares would be infinite, bound only by your views on the size and form of the universe.

6.02   Don't Fence Me In

1. Why design a new calculator? Don't such calculators already exist? Why a calculator? Why battery-powered? Why not solar-powered? Why just for accountants?

2. Why do you even need to design a can? Maybe the real problem is how to reduce the amount of garbage or how to recycle garbage.

3. Why just a door lock? What about windows? Why not redefine the problem in terms of how to keep people out of the house? Such a definition would expand greatly the number of possible solutions.

4. Why a telephone cord? Why not eliminate the cord entirely and use a wireless transmitter inside the house? Such products already are on the market.

5. Why do scissors have to be fatiguing? Why not electric scissors such as those that already exist? The definition of this problem may have to be restated to reflect what it is that you want to cut.

6.03   Create a New Viewpoint

One set of patterns can be found in the title of this exercise. These patterns are letters that form the word *CREATE*. If you had trouble seeing this word, don't worry. You're not alone. Some people even have to be guided, letter by letter, until they can make out the word. The other set of patterns are the shapes that outline the letters in *CREATE*.

What you have just experienced is an example of what psychologists refer to as figure-ground relationships. Because of the physical limitations of our brains, we only can observe one stimulus set at a time when contrasted against another. In this case, we can see either the word or the background patterns, but not both at the same time.

A well-developed mind should be able to switch back and forth from different patterns and relationships with relative ease. To test your ability to do this, try to focus on the word, then on the background patterns in rapid succession. If you can do this easily, you are well on the way to developing visual flexibility. If you have a little trouble in doing this, then all you need is more practice (assuming, of course, that you have no physical limitations).

6.04 Switch Around

This exercise requires you to analyze and synthesize figural information. The ability to do this rapidly is one sign of a flexible right brain, since spatial relationships are involved. What is required specifically in this situation is flexibility in the rotation of stimulus elements presented as visual figures. To solve the problem, each line is rotated one place to the left. Thus, the correct answer is *B*.

Some people have trouble with this exercise since the circles on the ends of the lines are not equidistant from one another. However, once the brain processes this bit of information, it is just a matter of determining the direction of the rotation.

6.05 Symbol Relatives

1,2,4,5,6,7,8,9,11	Have straight lines
2,4,6,7,11	Have only straight lines
1,3,5,8,9,10,12	Have curved lines
3,8,10,12	Have only curved lines
2,4,5,6,9,11	Have lines at right angles to each other
2,6,7,11	Have oblique angles
1,2,4,7,11	Have four or more straight lines
1,2,3,4,5,7,10,11,12	Have the same shape more than once
3,7,10,11,12	Represent common shapes (waves, hourglass, clouds, lightning, a flower)
1,3,4,5,6,7,8,12	Are symmetrical figures

6.06   Spy Telegrams

1. WAR, VETO
2. LIMBO, BORROW
3. BOMBAST, STOOL, TOOL
4. TOT, TULIPS, TULIP, LIPS
5. RUG, DAIS, SHOT
6. BUTTON, AGES
7. TON, TO, TABLE, ABLE, THERE, ETHER, HERE, HER
8. FILTER, BLEED
9. WON, CREATE, EAT, TEA
10. MONTH, PASTORALLY, PASTORAL, PASTOR, ORALLY, ORAL, OR, HEP, PAST

6.07   Breakdown

Some sample breakdowns are shown in Figures 6.7 and 6.8. There are many other possibilities, and you probably were able to come up with some of them. If you had trouble breaking down the figures, keep trying. You just need to persevere a little more or change your approach. For example, you might try darkening each line as you go along until you have included all of the lines in your breakdown.

6.08   Take a Stand

The "correct" answer to this problem is based on the placement of the newspaper. If the paper is placed in a doorway, then two people standing on either end of the paper would be unable to touch each other when the door is closed. See if you can stretch your right brain a little more and think of other possible solutions. Why not just tear the paper in half and move the pieces far away so that touching is impossible? Another solution would be to leave the paper as it is and inject both people with a paralyzing drug that would prevent all movement. What other creative solutions can you think of?

Figure 6.7 Some Possible Breakdowns of Drawing B

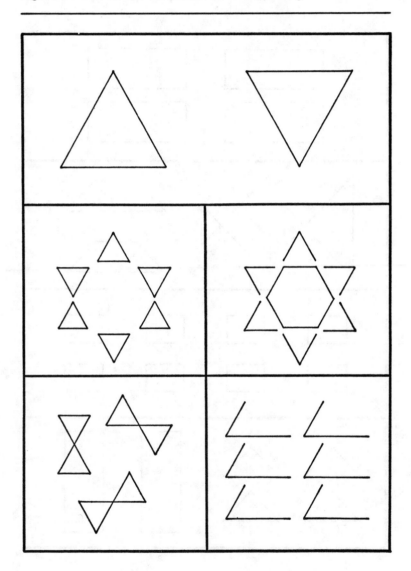

Figure 6.8 Some Possible Breakdowns of Drawing C

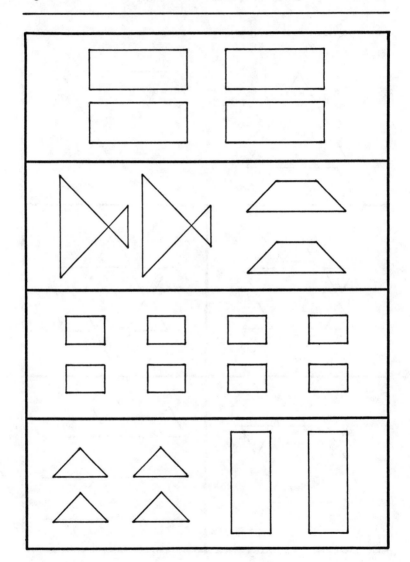

6.09   Take It Off

Slowly begin rolling one end of the rug toward the bottle. When the rug reaches the bottle, it will gradually push the bottle toward the other end of the rug until it slides off. The key to this exercise is to view the rug as a tool and not as just a floor covering.

However, it also might be possible to solve this problem without using the rug. Try to think of ways this might be possible. For example, could you use some type of vacuum device to pick up the bottle just enough to move it off the rug? Or, could you build a mold around the rug, cover the rug with a silicone gel, fill the mold with cement, and then slide the rug out from underneath the bottle? See if you can think of any other possible solutions.

6.10   Just Like That

1. Brushing your teeth is like:
   a. shining your shoes
   b. scrubbing the kitchen floor
   c. polishing silver
   d. washing your car
2. Disposing of garbage is like:
   a. getting a divorce
   b. going to the bathroom
   c. draining dirty bathwater
   d. spitting
3. Employee absenteeism is like:
   a. going on a vacation
   b. playing hooky from school
   c. having missing teeth
   d. having a meeting by yourself
4. Saving energy is like:
   a. putting money in the bank
   b. storing fat in your body
   c. being constipated
   d. an athlete resting between races

5. Driving a car is like:
   a. flying an airplane
   b. being a dictator
   c. being a matador
   d. steering a boat
6. School vandalism is like:
   a. a bombed-out city
   b. a boxing match
   c. an infectious disease
   d. a hawk hunting at night
7. Littering of the highways is like:
   a. having a broken garbage-disposal unit
   b. target shooting
   c. an ocean liner dumping its garbage
   d. a lawn water sprinkler
8. Job dissatisfaction is like:
   a. an unhappy marriage
   b. eating a bad meal
   c. buying a defective product
   d. finding a cockroach in your soup
9. Painting a house is like:
   a. putting on clothes
   b. covering a cake
   c. drinking fluoridated water
   d. getting a skin transplant
10. Cleaning a house is like:
    a. flushing a toilet
    b. picking lint off your coat
    c. a rainstorm
    d. leaves falling off a tree

When you develop analogies, you don't need to worry about whether or not the analogous activities are "correct" or bear a direct relationship to the original statement. The major purpose for developing analogies is to gain a new perspective on the problem. In doing so, you will be helping to break away from any constraints you may have placed on yourself or the problem.

Nevertheless, you will have to examine each analogy to see what solutions it might suggest. This activity of examining analogies and trying to develop practical solutions is known as a force fit. For example, the analogy that saving energy is like putting money in the bank might suggest the idea of using a battery. In this case, the energy can be stored when not needed, but withdrawn when it is.

Unfortunately, many people fail to take full advantage of the power residing in analogies and end up using direct analogies that often result in very conventional solutions. Although it is not always possible to do so, you should try to make most of your analogies as different as possible from the original statement of the problem.

6.11 SDRAWKCAB

1. How to make meetings more inefficient.
   How to make meetings more chaotic.
   How to make individuals more efficient.
   How to make individuals more inefficient.
   Possible Solutions: Allow time for unrestricted discussions, airing of grievances, etc. Or, a discussion on the way individuals organize their time and activities might be used to make meetings more organized.
2. How to decrease employee job satisfaction.
   How to increase employee job dissatisfaction.
   How to increase satisfaction with one's personal life.
   How to decrease satisfaction with one's personal life.
   Possible Solutions: Institute a suggestion program or increase participation in decision making.
3. How to increase street crime.
   How to increase charity on the street.
   How to decrease charity on the street.
   How to increase crime in the home.
   How to decrease crime in the home.
   Possible Solutions: Install emergency phone boxes on every street corner, or develop a citizen's crime-watch program.

4. How to increase arson.
   How to burn down every building in town.
   How to increase water damage to buildings.
   How to decrease water damage to buildings.
   Possible Solutions: Construct fireproof buildings
      or build them underwater or underground.
5. How to cause football injuries.
   How to prevent baseball injuries.
   How to cause baseball injuries.
   How to make football players avoid each other.
   Possible Solutions: Mandate wearing of highly
      impact-resistant pads or develop more restrictive
      rules for situations that cause the most injuries.

6.12   Would You Believe?

Original Objective	Exaggerated Objective	Possible Solution
Economical	No cost to use	Solar-powered; will pay for itself in two years
Fits on desk top	No desk space wasted	Recessed into desk
Produces thirty copies per minute	Produces fifty copies per minute	Adjustable copy rate
Minimal servicing	Servicing needed every day	Servicing can be done by user except for six-month checkups

6.13   Fantasyland

Fantasy Solutions	Practical Solutions
1. Eliminate all drivers.	Install a buried cable beneath the highway to control traffic.

2. Typewriter knows what you intend to type and self-corrects errors.

Typewriter types using a voice-actuated mechanism programmed to detect and correct errors.

3. Put the houses on a boat.

Build houses with inflatable airbags.

4. The carpet automatically cleans itself whenever dirt lands on it.

Use special built-in chemicals or a vacuum suction system built under the carpet.

5. Build a tire that doesn't use air or is self-inflating

Use a material that will provide the same comfort as air-filled tires but doesn't use air (such a tire currently is under development); make the tire porous and use a mechanism that will help regenerate the tire's air supply.

6.14   Silly Inventions

One type of silly invention would be a new type of bathroom scale with the following characteristics:

1. Whenever you step on the scale, you will weigh whatever weight you desire.

2. If you are overweight, as soon as you step on the scale, it will say "Ouch!"

3. Instead of you standing on the scale, you find out your weight by placing the scale on your head.

4. If you are overweight and start to eat something you shouldn't, the scale will automatically sense it and sound an alarm.

5. The scale will be so light in weight that you can take it with you in your suitcase on trips.

6. If you are overweight and begin to step on the scale, you will receive a mild electrical shock just as

your feet touch the top of the scale. You will continue to receive this shock until your weight is reduced to a figure programmed into the scale.

7. The scale will automatically record every weight registered, to be recalled on command.

Other examples of silly inventions might include a device that will activate electronically controlled objects using thought waves, or a sound-wave machine that will prevent any dust from collecting in a house.

6.15   *Just Suppose*

To do this exercise, you might begin by describing all the different aspects of this environment and activities that might be performed within it. For example, you might list doors, windows, TVs, lights, toilets, thermostats, refrigerators, ovens, blenders, vacuum cleaners, dishwashers, clothes washers, dryers, etc. Then you could consider the activities involved in using these items, as well as any other activities you might think of.

Because you are limited to just one finger, various types of electronic devices would be an obvious solution to most of the problems you would encounter. However, not all problems could be solved with electronics using existing technology. For example, how would you push a vacuum cleaner around, load clothes into a washing machine and fold them when dry, or cook a meal when you are limited to one finger? To solve these problems, you would have to design a new type of vacuum cleaner, for example, or come up with a completely new way of removing dirt and other particles from floors and carpets. Electronics may not always be the best way to solve this problem or similar ones.

7

LETTING GO

Pick up a pen or pencil and, without making any evaluations, think of ten different uses for it other than writing. Give yourself one minute to do this. Don't read any further until you have done it.

Finished? Did you come up with the different uses within the time period? The reason I asked you to do this exercise was to see how much power I could wield through the written word. If you complied without reading any further, I'd now like you to send me one hundred dollars. Just kidding. Honest (well, let me think about it).

The *real* reason for this little exercise was to demonstrate ideational fluency—the ability to generate large numbers of ideas with relative ease. Because creative solutions can't be judged as to their correctness, large numbers of ideas must be produced to increase the odds that at least one will lead to a satisfactory solution. Thus, the better you are at rapidly producing ideas, the more likely it is that you will come up with creative solutions. This is a basic principle of creativity.

There also are other types of fluency that may not be as well-known as ideational fluency. For example, there is word fluency and associational fluency. These two types are similar in that they are concerned with generating ideas, the backbone of the creative problem-solving process. They differ only in the manner in which they are used. Word fluency, for instance, involves rapid generation of words according to some specified symbolic requirement, such as words containing the letter *r*. Associational fluency, in contrast, uses rapid generation of words within a prescribed set of meaning—for example, a listing of synonyms.

Most of the fifteen exercises in this chapter are representative of the three types of fluency just described. Other exercises are representative of abilities closely related to general fluency. Most notable among these abilities are semantic spontaneous flexibility (rapid generation of ideas measured according to the categories of ideas produced) and figural spontaneous flexibility (being able to observe rapid changes in visual figures). They all, however, require you to rapidly produce ideas while suspending all judgment. Evaluation will come later, so concentrate only on being spontaneous and free in your responses.

7.01   Brain Gusher

A clogged-up brain can be a serious drawback when it comes to generating ideas. You must be able to let go and allow ideas to flow as rapidly as possible. Such fluency does not come easily, however, when the mind is blocked by censors that are geared to screening out right from wrong. There is nothing wrong with having these censors. But you must learn when the appropriate time exists for applying them.

Try to do the exercise that follows without using your censors. Just let the ideas flow out easily. Before you begin, get as relaxed as you can. Temporarily rid yourself of any problems that may be bothering you. Take several deep breaths. Inhale through your nose and exhale through your mouth. Feel the tension drain away.

Cover up all but the first word in the list of words that follows. Look at this word and write down the first three words that come to mind. Don't bother evaluating these words, just write them down as fast as you can think of them. Then uncover the second word and do the same thing with it. Continue in this manner until you have completed the exercise, using all fifty words.

hope	red	tape	wood	laugh
star	square	rocket	money	paper
glass	dry	flower	egg	silly
early	book	cork	horse	train
never	menace	happy	out	snow
pig	free	fence	fat	walk
card	water	old	hard	late
light	yesterday	near	cold	above
dog	balloon	ride	ant	cow
moon	elbow	mountain	rough	help

7.02   Prefix-It

As an exercise in word fluency, practice doing the following: As rapidly as possible, list as many words as you can think of in two minutes that begin with the prefix *dis*. Now do the same thing for the prefixes *anti* and *con*.

7.03   Letter Hunt

One variation of the Prefix-It exercise involves listing as many words as possible (in two minutes) that contain a specified letter of the alphabet. Try this exercise for each of the following letters: *g*, *k*, *p*.

7.04   Underweight

As another test of your fluency skills, list everything you can think of that weighs less than a pound. Do this as quickly as possible and stop after three minutes.

7.05   Word Chains

Associational fluency is an important aspect of creativity. Use this exercise to see how well you can make connections among words, even though they are unrelated, to describe another word.

Using the following word clusters, try to think of at least two different objects that each cluster could describe.

1. metal
   hinged
   attaches
2. wire
   talk
   plastic
3. paper
   glue
   ink
4. keys
   rubber
   letters

5. fabric
   foam
   floor
6. dirt
   green
   water
7. soft
   white
   paper
8. rectangular
   flat
   metal

7.06   Sniff Out

There are thousands of people who suffer from allergies. Many of these people receive desensitizing injections of medicine drawn from small glass vials. I happen to be one of the people affected in this manner and receive two injections every week. The nurse who provides me with this thrill either disposes of the empty bottles or gives them to me.

I use up about one hundred of these little bottles every year. If only five thousand other people use the same number of bottles, that amounts to a half-million bottles each year, most of which probably are thrown away. Even if some are reused for the same purpose, a large number of bottles still would be wasted. Now, if similar wasteful activities occur with other products, the amount of energy consumed to produce such disposables must be staggering. Help me solve this problem by doing the following:

> Think of ("sniff out") how many different ways these bottles might be used once they have been emptied of their contents. A drawing of one of the bottles, along with relevant information, is presented in Figure 7.1.

Figure 7.1 Specifications for Allergy Medicine Vials

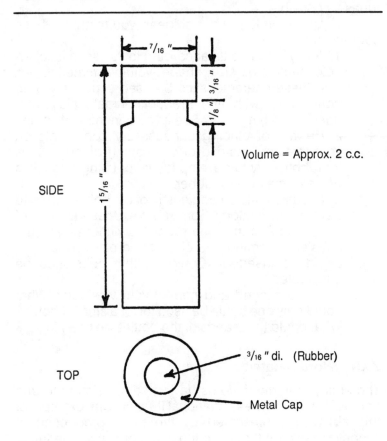

To perform this exercise, first write down all the different uses that you can think of within five minutes. Then go do something else for about ten minutes. Return and list ideas for about five more minutes.

Were your ideas unique the second time? Not all of them may seem practical at the time you think of them, but you shouldn't let this worry you now. Any evaluation of your ideas can come later. Right now, the important thing is to put blinders on your critical eye and come up with as many ideas as possible.

If you begin to run out of ideas, you might try these suggestions:

1. Analyze the bottle according to its essential characteristics, e.g., size, shape, volume, material, etc. Can these characteristics be used separately or in combination with other products or materials to produce something new? See if you can think of some.

2. Beware of placing unnecessary constraints on your thinking. Instead of developing different uses for a bottle, try to develop ideas for using quantities of glass, metal, and rubber.

3. Focus on one characteristic of the bottle and try to develop an analogy. For example, does insertion of the syringe through the rubber to withdraw a liquid substance remind you of anything else? What else could be inserted? Could another substance be substituted?

4. Try to expand and narrow your viewpoint. What could only one bottle be used for, or a smaller bottle? What could thousands of the bottles be used for?

7.07   Word Relatives

The ability to think of words having some relation to one another is known as associational fluency. One example of this ability is represented by the rapid production of synonyms—words that have the same or similar meaning.

For example, two synonyms for the word joyful would be elated and glad. For each of the words that follow, think of as many synonyms as you can within one minute.

shout   hit
even   make
decide   see

7.08   Gar·bägé

Select five items that might be found in a wastebasket or garbage can and generate ten different uses for each item as fast as you can. Don't worry about how original or practical your ideas may seem. For this exercise, you should be concerned only with generating uses as rapidly as possible, even if they seem a little bit silly. If you can do this very quickly, then you probably are very good at ideational fluency.

7.09   Go to Class

This variation of exercises involving generation of different uses for an object requires you to do the same thing, but with one change. Instead of randomly listing uses for an object, list only uses that belong to a particular class of objects. Then think of another class and list uses for it. To illustrate, a listing of different uses for a red brick might involve such classes as construction, weights, or support systems. To be useful, you should try to do this exercise as rapidly as possible.

Practice this skill by quickly listing uses and classes for a wire coat hanger. List the class first, followed by all the different uses you can think of. Then go on to the next class and list all the uses you can think of for it. Continue this activity until you run out of classes.

7.10   Don't Forget

A mnenomic device is something that can be used to help memorize lists of data or information. When trying to memorize a list of objects, for example, many people will take the first letter of the first word for each item and construct a sentence. Usually this sentence is one that doesn't make much sense, although it can be very helpful in recalling the entire list by making associations between the words and the objects. To illustrate, the following sentence might be constructed from a grocery list containing the words potato, celery, sugar, and eggs: Please Call Sam Early.

Practice your fluency skills by seeing how many different sentences you can construct from the word *mnemonic.* Do this as rapidly as possible for about five minutes. By the way, it is usually easier to recall silly sentences than it is more logical ones, so don't be concerned if your sentences don't make much sense.

7.11   Column Relatives

This exercise will help you in developing associational fluency.

From the columns below, select one word from the first column and one word from the second column. Then identify as many things as possible that possess these two attributes. For example, something hot and mobile might be a hair dryer, a jet engine, or the sun.

Try to use at least ten different two-word combinations. Once you have mastered these, try it with one word from the first column and two words from the second. If you can do this easily and rapidly, give your right brain a little pat.

hot	mobile
cold	silvery
large	wooden
small	metallic

fast	electrical
slow	glass
square	slippery
round	rough
expensive	transparent
inexpensive	flexible

7.12   Just Alike, Only Different

The ability to develop common associations among apparently unrelated objects or concepts is an important skill in creative thinking. It is the recognition of such common associations that very often leads to the development of creative solutions.

See how many different areas of commonality you can think of for the words that follow. (There is really no such thing as a correct answer to this exercise.) Begin gradually by looking for areas of common ground between pairs of words. Then progress by adding one word at a time until you are working with at least four different words. Any combination of words will do, so don't feel restricted to just rows or columns.

dime	tree	square	telephone
book	window	bucket	paint
airplane	city	pencil	rug
egg	garden	flashlight	flower

As an example, a dime and a rug both can be rolled, while an egg, window, and flower all can be broken rather easily.

7.13   It Came From Beneath the Blot

The ability to assign labels to ambiguous material can provide a useful exercise in increasing mental fluency. Although originality also is required for such an exercise, the ease with which you can produce labels will provide a fair indication of how fluent you are.

Using the ink-blot pattern shown in Figure 7.2, make up ten possible titles for a movie the pattern might represent.

Figure 7.2 Ink Blot for Developing Movie Titles

7.14 What's in a Name?

This exercise provides practice in an associational fluency skill that is highly developed in many bureaucrats: the ability to replace simple, easily understood names with more complex and vague names. For instance, a teacher might be called a language-skills coordinator, a janitor a custodial engineer, and a store clerk a goods-exchange facilitator.

Practice your associational fluency by making up bureaucratic-sounding titles for the following occupations:

plumber	dentist	disc jockey
baker	lawyer	house painter
doctor	bus driver	undertaker

Don't try to be too bureaucratic when making up your titles. Silly, nonbureaucratic names are OK, too.

7.15   Spy Stories

Although this exercise will test your originality, it also will provide you with practice in making associations between words.

Using at least one secret code word from each telegram in the Spy Telegrams exercise, write a brief spy story. Just to make things a little more interesting, use the words in the order in which they appeared in the different telegrams. Don't spend a lot of time thinking about what to write or how to write it. Just let your thoughts flow naturally.

COMMENTS AND SAMPLES

7.01   Brain Gusher

How much trouble did you have with this exercise? Did the words flow easily, or did you find yourself stumbling to think of words? If you hesitated very much when thinking of words, your censors probably were getting in your way. It can take some practice to do this exercise effortlessly. If you think you need some more practice, try it again.

You also might want to think about why you came up with the words you did. You may find a clue in your experiential background that will provide you with more insight into how you come up with ideas. Such awareness can be very helpful when looking for ways to become more creative.

7.02   Prefix-It

The following illustrate words beginning with the prefixes, *dis*, *anti*, and *con*.

dis	*anti*	*con*
disassociate	antibiotic	contract
disapprove	antibody	concave
disappear	anticlimax	conceal
disallow	antidote	concede
disappoint	antifreeze	conceit
discourage	antihistamine	conceive
disband	antimatter	concentrate
disarm	antipasto	concentric
disable	antipathy	concept
disadvantage	antiquated	concern
disagree	antiseptic	concert
disassemble	antisocial	concession
disavow	antithesis	conciliate
discard	antitoxic	concise
discharge	antidisestab-	conclude
	lishmentarianism	

7.03   Letter Hunt

If most or all of your words began with the specified letter, try this exercise again—only this time, try to use words in which the specified letter is not the first letter of the word. If you want to make it even harder, avoid using words that rhyme.

Once you have completed this exercise, think back on how you prompted your mind to think of the words. If you used a system of some sort, you probably could do this with little effort. For example, you could have systematically looked over all the objects in your immediate environment or progressed through the letters of the alphabet.

7.04   Underweight

Here's a list of items typically generated by persons doing this exercise:

1. butterfly	16. checkbook
2. canary	17. comb
3. hummingbird	18. strand of hair
4. feather	19. button
5. pen	20. shoelace
6. pencil	21. sugar cube
7. paper clip	22. grain of salt
8. leaf	23. piece of bread
9. blade of grass	24. light bulb
10. piece of paper	25. eraser
11. watch	26. pillow
12. sock	27. playing card
13. tie	28. staple
14. envelope	29. Kleenex
15. stamp	30. driver's license

You should have listed at least thirty different items. If you didn't, think of how you went about getting ideas. One way to increase your fluency on such tasks is to think of classes of objects and list items contained within each. For example, you might think of different kinds of birds, foods, clothing, etc. If you feel the need to practice some more, do so until you can list fifty or more items with little trouble. To be fair, use different items every time you make a list.

7.05 *Word Chains*

1. Stapler or door
2. Telephone, walkie-talkie, or tape recorder.
3. Book, party hat, envelope, or decorated paper straw.
4. Typewriter, typesetting machine, or initialed key ring with rubber decoration.
5. Chair, couch, or floor pillow.
6. Plant, child's green trousers after playing outside, green truck in a car wash, or garden hose stuck in the grass.
7. Kleenex, toilet paper, white cat with a paper collar, or package of cotton.
8. Table, door, cookie sheet, or window screen. The list is almost limitless on this one.

7.06 *Sniff Out*

1. Milk bottle for dollhouse
2. Paint container
3. Smooth putty in small places
4. Drawing a small circle
5. Fill with volcanic dust and sell
6. Perfume bottle
7. Prop up a window
8. Make a musical instrument
9. Wind chimes
10. Recycle with other glass products
11. A small doll
12. Earrings
13. Cuff links
14. Display for insects
15. Biological cultures
16. Small pulley
17. Glue together to make a fountain pen
18. Weight for a clock
19. Beaded curtains
20. Miniature ships
21. Christmas-tree decorations
22. Target practice
23. Fishing float
24. Necklace

25. Toy baby bottles
26. Egg timer
27. Light bulb
28. Erasers
29. Buttons
30. Salt and pepper shakers
31. Cigarette filter
32. Rubber chair stops
33. Reflective material for highways
34. Single-letter rubber stamps
35. Advertise wine samples
36. Explosive caps
37. Miniature bowling game
38. Glass sculptures
39. Ashtrays
40. Oxygen tanks

Do these ideas suggest any others? Can you modify or combine any of these to create new objects?

7.07 Word Relatives

Shout: cry out, hoot, exclaim, vociferate, yell

Even: level, flat, smooth, regular, steady, equal, balanced, fair

Decide: determine, settle, resolve, purpose, conclude

Hit: strike, collide, clash, blow, stroke

Make: form, build, produce, fabricate, create, construct, manufacture, fashion, mold, shape, cause, render, constitute, transform, convert

See: perceive, look at, spy, notice, discern, observe, view, watch.

7.08 Gar•bägé

Here are five different items and examples of possible uses for each:

Styrofoam egg carton: packing material, hold small items, Christmas tree ornaments, wall covering, toy igloos, toy cars, bird feeder, funny eyeglasses, sugar scoops, wall insulation.

Tin can: pencil holder, paintbrush holder, pot for small

plants, cement mold, bait pail, toy telephones, camping shower, camping stove, dollhouse roof, birdhouse

Foil: sun reflector, cooking, birdcage lining, TV antenna, window caulking, space suit for mice, insulated socks, model-airplane covering, cape for "foil man" costume, disco bathing suit

Paper napkins: paper hat, toy parachute, ink blotter, place-mats, earplugs, party decorations, tent for snails, doll dress, disposable bandit masks

Envelope: coupon holder, scrap-paper holder, frog sleeping bag, hat for ice cream vendor, swing seat for chipmunks, earmuffs, portable toilet for pigeons, use to mail grass clippings and dog "residue" to your best enemy, attaché case for ferrets, ant bag for pet ants.

7.09 *Go To Class*

Using five classes, here are some possible uses of a coat hanger:

Food: shish kebab, hot dogs, marshmallows, chestnuts, popcorn holder

Holding things: key rings, flowerpots, hanging pictures, paper-towel holder, spools of thread, bucket handle, plants, fish stringer, shoe rack, tie rack, kitchen utensils

Decorations: mobiles, bracelet, Christmas-tree ornaments, wreaths, sculptures, earrings

Holding in hands: back scratcher, drain unclogger, fire poker, fishing pole, pointer for lectures, pipe cleaner

Repairs: auto mufflers, chains, bicycle spokes, antennas, broken-bone splint, umbrellas

7.10 *Don't Forget*

Meet Nat Every Monday Over New Income Costs.

Maybe Nellie Eats Moose On Naked Indian Calves.

Must Newton Eat Money Over Nancy's Ice Cupboard?

Mutts Near Egbert Mean Only Ned Is Coming.

Missiles Need Energy Material Or Nuclear Incidents Collapse.

Move Near Every Mother On Narcotics In Cans.

Multiplying Nuts Envelop Mice Over Nice Icky Clouds.

Make Ned's Enormous Muscles Of Nitrous Indian Clay.

Magic Norton Exchanges Monkeys Outside Nets In Clusters.

Mike Noticed Eggs Mom Organized Neatly In Concert.

7.11   Column Relatives

hot-mobile: hog-dog vendor's cart, an elephant's breath, a lighted cigar being thrown into a trash can.

cold-silvery: coins on a cold day, someone wearing a silver ring putting their hand in a freezer, an outdoor thermometer during the winter.

large-wooden: a tree, a building, a wooden sculpture, a wooden bridge.

small-metalic: a dime, a paper clip, a thumbtack.

fast-electrical: a high-speed train, a neon light, a watch, a clothes iron falling out of a window.

slow-glass: marbles used by someone with only two fingers, windows on a car stalled in heavy traffic.

square-slippery: a newly waxed floor tile, a wet sidewalk, a block of ice.

round-rough: a used croquet ball, a porcupine in a fetal position, a man with a crew cut and an unshaven face.

expensive-transparent: a diamond, crystal stemware, gasoline.

inexpensive-flexible: rubber bands, straws, taffy, chewing gum.

7.12   Just Alike, Only Different

Here are just a few of the many commonalities possible using two-, three-, and four-word combinations:

dime-tree: both are round, have rough outer edges, can be recycled, and are capable of growing in value over time.

book-window: both transmit information, are made of plane shapes, and can be opened and closed.

egg-bucket: both can carry different substances, can be bought in a store, and are found on many farms.

pencil-rug-flower: all three are or can be made of natural materials, can be found in a house, and can be used for decorative purposes.

airplane-garden-flashlight: all three contain something, can be round in shape, and involve some type of movement.

city-square-telephone-dime: all four involve exchanges between or among people, are relevant to the communications media, and have prescribed boundaries.

7.13   It Came from Beneath the Blot

Examples of different titles include:
1. Cosmic Frog
2. Mating of the Platypuses
3. The Women with the Silly Hats
4. They Wore Poodles on Their Heads
5. Journey into the Void
6. Black Curse of the Albino Rats

7. The Squashing of the Toads
8. Bonzo Gets a Hickey
9. Flying Arrowships
10. Saga of the Gorilla Janitors

To make full use of the different stimuli provided by this blot, you should view it from different angles. You also should switch back and forth from the figure-ground relationships presented by dark and white contrasts.

If you only use one perspective, then your fluency level will be greatly diminished. Note that the same principle also holds true when you are faced with an unstructured problem situation. You must be able to view situations from many different perspectives if you want to produce unique solutions.

7.14   What's in a Name?

plumber: suction supervisor, tube technician, faucet facilitator, waste-products programmer, flushologist.

baker: leavening leader, yeast specialist, dough blower, input preparer, rising-materials diagnostician.

doctor: body checker, organ analyst, pill-prescriber technician, sickness-assessment counselor, body-reviver specialist.

dentist: hired gum, drill biller, drill sergeant, manual incisor-extraction specialist, oral manipulator.

lawyer: legal-litigator analyst, court-presentation specialist, legal-scripture interpreter, tort technician, liability-liaison coordinator.

bus driver: commuter controller, wheeled-conveyor operator, person-movement facilitator, token receiver, mass-movement manager.

disc jockey: disc dealer, flatter-platter player, tune technician, spinologist, aural augmenter.

house painter: exterior-application artist, coating special-ist, brush master, appearance manipulator, drip spreader.

undertaker: permanent-resident specialist, plot-placement analyst, underground agent, rigor mortis manager, corpus planter.

7.15   Spy Stories

War is never a pleasant experience, Harry Curtain thought as he made his way to George Elbow's tent to *borrow* a razor blade. Walking into the tent, Harry pulled up a *stool* to sit on and moistened his *lips.*

"Did you find out yet who *shot* K.R.?" said Harry as he eyed the top *button* on George's coat.

"No," replied George, "we haven't been able to deter-mine when he was shot."

"Well, we now know that he did *bleed* to death, as was originally thought."

George looked surprised at this revelation. "Do you think someone set out to *create* the impression that he had not bled to death?"

Harry nodded in agreement and looked *past* George to the blood-stained razor on Harry's dresser. "Yeah, I definitely think that's what happened, and it wasn't the *pastor* who did it."

BEING DIFFERENT

Originality probably is the one aspect of creativity about which most people feel the least confident. A natural tendency is to compare the creative products of others with those we have produced ourselves. Such comparisons are fine except when we use them to put ourselves down. In such instances, we usually have set an unrealistic standard for ourselves. We expect that we should be able to do many things as well as the people we admire. We fail to recognize, however, that each one of us is unique and creative in our own way.

Although we might be able to increase our originality in terms of variety of ideas produced, we still retain our basic uniqueness. To expect that we should be as unique as everyone else is unrealistic and redundant. If we all were alike in our originality, then no one would be unique or original. In fact, by definition, we all could not be alike in

139

our originality since we would have no one with whom to compare ourselves.

So cherish your own uniqueness and originality. Don't try to be someone you're not. But do try to build on and increase your own originality. Forget what everyone else can do. Learn basic skills and perspectives from others, but then go off on your own. You can make your own little contribution to the world just by being yourself.

The fifteen exercises that follow will provide you with an opportunity to practice your originality in a variety of ways. There are exercises dealing with figural elaboration, product modifications and improvements, symbolic redefinitions, development of new names, and story completions.

When doing these exercises, you should not be too concerned with how unique your responses are. Your major goal, instead, should be to express your own uniqueness to the fullest extent possible. Stretch your imagination as much as you can, but don't worry about whether or not someone else could do the exercises better than you. You are trying to train *your* creative mind, not someone else's.

8.01 Steaming Ideas

Do you ever get steamed about something? For example, do you get irritated with a desk-top telephone that slides all over the place while you're using it and eventually falls on the floor right when that special someone is proposing marriage or some other desirable event? Or, what about those cellophane packages that different foods come in? Have you ever loosened a tooth trying to tear one open when no sharp objects were available? Well, if you have experienced any of these and other similar irritants of everyday life, you are ready for this exercise.

Think of things in your environment that really get you steamed. Make a list and then select the five items that bug you the most. What improvements could be made? For example, could the so-called "resealable" waxed paper found in most cereal boxes be integrated somehow with the box top so that it doesn't remain unfolded when not in use? Think of as many different solutions as you can for each of the five items on your list.

8.02   Fill-Out

Many problems present only partial information to the problem solver. The ability to build on incomplete information is a skill needed of all problem solvers, especially those faced with unstructured problems. A creative element exists in such situations since the elaborations made to solve the problem usually cannot be evaluated in terms of their correctness.

This exercise will provide you with practice in visual elaboration of figures. When working on these figures, keep in mind that the unconventional response is likely to be the most creative.

Complete the following figures:

$$\sqrt{} \qquad \omega \qquad C$$

8.03   Draw-a-Word

We usually communicate our thoughts in words and, much less often, in pictures. We could communicate more vividly, however, if we would use both words and pictures. Practice your originality by making pictures out of words. To get you started, here are two examples:

Now try it yourself with these words: cash, telephone, radio, elevators. Want more practice? Make pictures of as many words as you can from the following paragraph:

The letter arrived by airmail on Thursday. It offers the first look at the administration's priorities as the university prepares to trim its budget needs to meet expected levels of funding.

8.04　Picture That

The ability to depict information in different forms can be a valuable asset to creative problem solving. Test this aspect of your creativity by completing the exercise that follows.

You have been commissioned by the New Product Association to produce information signs for their international exhibit. Because not everyone who will be attending the exhibit understands English, you will need to develop symbols that indicate the direction of a product area, but without using words. For example, signs for rest rooms might be designed this way:

(Men)　　　　(Women)

The major product areas are:

1. typewriters	11. plumbing supplies
2. telephones	12. lighting
3. bicycles	13. tires
4. televisions	14. watches
5. calculators	15. lawn mowers
6. automobiles	16. golf equipment
7. skis	17. cameras
8. sailboats	18. suitcases
9. tanks	19. electric fans
10. airplanes	20. hair dryers

8.05   Something New

The different characteristics of ideas often can be used to suggest new ideas, objects, or improvements.

For this exercise you will need to select an object or idea, break it down by describing its different features, and then modify these features to suggest something new. A hand-held egg beater, for example, could be broken down and modified as follows:

1. handle   trigger grip; lengthen with counter-weights
2. crank   make larger
3. gears   increase ratio
4. beaters   coat with nonstick substance

Try doing the same thing for the following objects or use your own: electric can opener, blender, toaster.

8.06   Grid Lock

One systematic method frequently used to generate a large number of ideas is based on the principle of forced relationships. This principle simply involves forcing together two or more objects or ideas to produce new ones. One variant of this procedure uses object characteristics to produce new ideas.

From the grid in Figure 8.1, select an object from the first column and then one of the two attributes from each of the remaining columns. Using the attributes you have selected, develop a new variation of the object.

8.07   Label It

Labels play an important role in creativity since they either can restrict or enlarge our perceptual boundaries. For example, we call a plane figure with four equal sides at right angles to each other a square. And, as shown in Figure 8.2, we can very simply represent this label by

Figure 8.1 Grid for Producing Object Variations

OBJECTS

Chair	Table	Ladder	Bookcase	Lamp	Bed	Workbench	Desk	
								Metal / Wood
								Glass / Plastic
								Long / Short
								Round / Square
								Light / Heavy
								Tall / Short
								Movable / Fixed
								Single-purpose / Multi-purpose
								Narrow / Wide
								Hard / Soft
								Comes apart / Unitary
								Electrical / Nonelectrical
								One color / Many colors

ATTRIBUTES

drawing four lines that conform to our definition of a square.

However, we also can represent a square by the space it occupies. Thus, instead of drawing lines, we can fill in the space surrounding the lines, as is represented in Figure 8.3.

Figure 8.2 Plane Figure With Four Equal Sides at Right Angles to Each Other

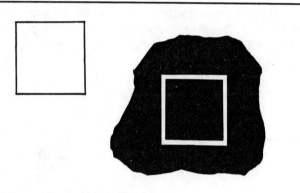

Figure 8.3 Example of a Squarinout

Now we have both bounded and unbounded space separated by a pattern that we traditionally have called a square. Note that this figure also conforms to our definition of what a square is. However, since we have altered our perceptual representation of this figure, it may no longer be appropriate to label it a square. Instead, we may want to call it a *squarinout*, for example. Thus, if we always call a square a square, we may limit ourselves in the conceptual tools we can bring to bear in solving a problem requiring creativity.

What other names can you think of for a square? To do this, think of the different ways that a square can be constructed or figures can be developed using shapes containing squares.

8.08   Light Up Your Life

The method of forced relationships has been widely used to produce new variations of a product or idea. Although there are many different versions of this method, one common one involves taking some object or idea unrelated to the object or idea you want to modify and forcing them together to suggest something new. For instance, a light bulb might be forced together with a chair to suggest a new type of chair that is made of glass or is bulb-shaped.

Use the products listed below to see how many different improvements you can make with each, using a light bulb as the unrelated object.

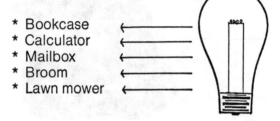

 * Bookcase
 * Calculator
 * Mailbox
 * Broom
 * Lawn mower

8.09   Word to Word

One way to produce new ideas is to reverse the procedure where an idea is developed and then given a name. That is, ideas also can be produced by starting with a name and then seeing what ideas might be suggested.

Use the words you formed from the Bunny Hop exercise to develop a new invention. For example, the word *bar* from *rabbit* and the word *it* from *multiply* could be combined to form Bar-It, a new type of door lock.

8.10   Name That Exercise

Develop a new name for all of the exercises in Chapters 4 through 10 in this book. Don't think too long on any one. Try to be spontaneous and as original as possible.

8.11   The Master

The air was heavy with anticipation as Ralph entered the large, marble-tiled room. At the other end, surrounded by cushions, parchment scrolls, and various brass objects, sat The Master. He seemed to be deep in thought, contemplating the mysteries of the universe. As Ralph drew closer he could sense the piercing eyes that seemed capable of cutting through one's soul yet embracing one warmly at the same time.

Now, at the foot of the Master's ornately carved wooden perch, Ralph waited for a sign that he could speak. The Master looked away and cleared his throat. Taking this for the sign, Ralph began, "Master ..." but was cut off as The Master raised his hand to signal silence. "Wrong sign," thought Ralph. Then The Master parted his mouth and began to speak, the words rolling slowly off his lips: "Yes, what do you want already?" With these words of encouragement, Ralph stammered and then blurted out the words that had haunted him for so many years now: "Master, why have we been placed here on earth?"

With eyes that had witnessed almost a century of the human drama, The Master lowered his gaze to the floor and spoke nothing for five minutes. Then, as if by divine inspiration, he raised his eyes and looked directly at Ralph. "Crumbs," he said, and as he did, a wry smile formed at the corners of his mouth.

What did The Master mean by "crumbs"?

8.12   End It All

Write a humorous ending for the story that follows. This exercise also can provide entertainment as a game when several others are involved. For example, after everyone has described an ending, the most humorous one could be selected and the person awarded a prize.

Greg stealthily crept down the long corridor as

the shadows from the wall torches danced lightly around him. It was cold and he wished that he had worn his long underwear. On his last two missions he had worn his long johns, only to find himself sweltering in some tropical climate. "Oh well," he thought, "life is knowing how to go on when you don't have your favorite pair of long johns."

Just then, his excursion into the deep philosophical issues of life was interrupted by a long, piercing scream, "Arrrrrrrgh!" He paused momentarily and sharpened his senses. Even without his long johns, he felt his legs begin to perspire and his pulse quicken. "What could that horrifying scream mean?" he thought. Had he finally found what he was sent to find?

"I must be careful now," he said to himself. The slightest error could make the difference between success and failure.

He padded quietly to the end of the corridor, where he was met by a large, wooden door. Instead of a conventional doorknob, however, this door had a large cast-iron ring for a handle. Before pulling on the ring, he paused. "What if the door creaks like in one of those B movies?" Well, that was just a risk he would have to take. Grasping the ring, he tugged with all his might. No creak. The door didn't budge. It was then that he saw the other decorative rings that also looked like door handles. So, *pushing* the door open, he peered inside. It was then that he first heard the voices.

As the sliver of light from the partially opened door bounced off the walls of the corridor, Greg strained to hear the voices. They were laughing, but only the laughs of someone who has just committed or was about to commit some heinous deed. Pushing the door open further, he peered in and saw for the first time what he had most feared. This is what he had come to find. For inside the room, he saw ...

8.13   Nasal Nonsense

This is another exercise for practicing originality. Your task: Write a humorous ending for the following story.

Cora looked up from her receptionist's desk at the Newtown Nasal Clinic just in time to see Dr. Sid Septum open the door to the supply room, cast a furtive glance up and down the hall, and quietly slip inside, closing the door behind him. She thought nothing of it, as the doctor often had to obtain nasal supplies from the room. However, when Nurse Sally Spray entered the room a few minutes later, her suspicions were aroused.

The good doctor and the nurse had been meeting like this for several months, and Cora was becoming more and more indignant. Sure, maybe her own nose was a little too small. But it was a nice nose. Her entire family had been cursed with small noses and she had almost resigned herself to her fate until she had met Dr. Snaffle several years ago.

She had been eating lunch one day near the bottom of the Spanish Steps in Rome when she had to blow her nose. Taking out a clean handkerchief from her purse, she carefully blew her nose. At almost the same moment, an attractive couple came walking down the steps and the man tripped over Cora's sack lunch. As he bent over to help her pick up the spilled contents, their eyes met and then their noses almost touched—her small protuberance and his more normal, elongated nose.

'Hi. I'm Harry Snaffle and I guess I've ruined your lunch. Would you care to join us? We were just on our way to have lunch ourselves."

Instinctively shrinking from his gesture of kindness because of her inferior nose, she hesitated and then reluctantly accepted. The pigeons were now beginning to gather around her spilled lunch, and she was still hungry. So Cora introduced herself to

Dr. Snaffle, Dr. Snaffle introduced Cora to his companion, Sally Spray, and they began walking together.

There was something about Sally that Cora didn't like. It could have been the way she seemed to look down her nose at Cora when she greeted her. Or it could have been the menacing way Sally seemed to peer into her eyes. Cora made a mental note to try and figure out later what it was about Sally that disturbed her.

Meanwhile, they continued to stroll along in the noonday sun. Soon they began to cross over the Bridge of Angels, and it was there that Cora first noticed Dr. Snaffle's magnificent profile. For there, silhouetted against the background of St. Peter's cathedral, was the biggest nose she had ever seen.

She continued to marvel at his nose over lunch and barely said a word the entire time. So she was taken by surprise when Dr. Snaffle offered her the receptionist's job at his nasal clinic back in the states.

As Cora reminisced about her chance meeting with Dr. Snaffle and Nurse Spray, she decided that it was time she took some action in regard to what she considered to be outrageous behavior on the part of Dr. Septum and Sally Spray.

She rose from her desk, smoothed down the wrinkles on her dress, and picked up her purse. Opening it, she rummaged around inside, pushed aside the handkerchiefs and nose sprays, and located her compact. Removing it from her purse, she opened it and took one last look in its mirror at her deficient proboscis.

She snapped the compact shut and tossed it on her desk. She then inhaled deeply, lowered her chin, and strode purposefully toward the supply-room door. Grasping the knob, she forcefully wrenched open the door and saw Dr. Septum examining Nurse Spray's ...

8.14   Pork Role

The ability to synthesize apparently unrelated bits of information to produce something new is an important aspect of creative functioning. This exercise will help to stretch your ability to produce original ideas and integrate them into meaningful patterns.

Assume that you are a writer for a magazine that features short stories. Your job has been to take story titles suggested by your boss and develop an appropriate narrative to fit. Recently you have been so successful at doing this that your boss has become a little envious. So she decides she will test your creative powers by giving you the following line: "When the string is long, the pig is short."

Using this statement, write a brief story that will be appropriate for the title.

8.15   Create That Exercise

For your "final exam" in originality, make up your own exercises for improving different aspects of creative thinking. Try to develop at least two exercises for Chapters 4 through 10.

COMMENTS AND SAMPLE ANSWERS

8.01   Steaming Ideas

Bug List	*Possible Solutions*
1. Items (e.g., pens, toys) sealed in molded plastic containers.	Use "Ziploc" packaging; use the same molding but with a foil backing for easy opening.
2. Childproof pill bottles	Use a combination dial: Turn cap to two specified numbers and cap comes off.
3. Shoes that don't quite fit	Use a material that conforms to the human foot. After wearing for a while, it can be "locked in" to the shape of the wearer's foot.
4. Unopened cans of auto oil covered with a coating of oil	Wrap cans in plastic bags; sell oil in double-thickness foil pouches with built-in pouring spout.
5. Grass that sticks to the underside of lawn mowers	Spray with antistick substance; have suction tubes continually remove grass; have blowers continually blowing grass away from underside of the mower.

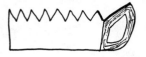

8.03   *Draw-A-Word*

Here are some sample drawings for the words. Yours might be completely different, which is OK since there are no right or wrong answers to this exercise.

CA$H

RADIO

TELE📞HONE

ELEVAToRS

The ⟦letter⟧ arrived by ◄A✈RMAIL on   M   T   W   (TH)
F   S   S. It offers the first LOOK at the administration's
① P ② R ③ I ④ O ⑤ R ⑥ I ⑦ T ⑧ I
⑨ E ⑩ S   as the UNIVERSITY prepares to TRIM
its budget needs to ME►◄ET expected $\frac{LE}{VELS}$ of
F$UNDING.

8.04 Picture That

1. typewriters

6. automobiles

2. telephones

7. skis

3. bicycles

8. sailboats

4. televisions

9. tanks

5. calculators

10. airplanes

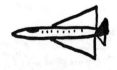

11. plumbing supplies

16. golf equipment

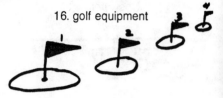

12. lighting

17. cameras

13. tires

18. suitcases

14. watches

19. electric fans

15. lawn mowers

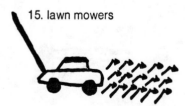

20. hair dryers

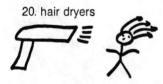

8.05   Something New

Electric Can Opener
1. Cutting disk   Make it reversible
2. Clamp   Make it wider; make it conform to the hand
3. Motor housing   Eliminate ridges to make it easier to clean
4. Magnet   Make it removable for cleaning

Blender
1. Container   Make it unbreakable
2. Blade   Thicken it or use stronger metal
3. Base   Widen it or add suction cups to bottom
4. Push buttons   Use a dial instead

Toaster
1. Heating elements   Make them movable to obtain desired degree of darkness
2. Lever   Eliminate; toast automatically enters toaster
3. Darkness control   Adapt to adjust distance of heating elements from the toast
4. Housing   Make it transparent

8.06   Grid Lock

Using a chair as the object, the following attributes might be selected:

wood	multipurpose
plastic	wide
long	soft
round	comes apart
light	electrical
tall	many colors
movable	

With these attributes, a chair could be designed that has a wooden frame, uses molded or pliable plastic for the seat, is relatively long, has rounded edges, is light in weight, is designed especially for tall people, can be easily moved, has several different purposes, is extra wide, is soft to sit in, is easily disassembled, has electrical devices to serve its various functions, and comes in a variety of colors. For instance, the chair might be electrically moved to different sitting positions, instantly mold to the sitter's body (something like a bean-bag chair), double as a seat for a car or as a lawn chair, vibrate, dispense drinks, etc.

8.07   Label It

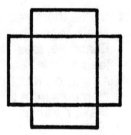

1. Backtangle—from the "backs" of four rectangles

2. Boxrim—from the top edge of a square box

3. Di-arrow—two arrows joined together at their base

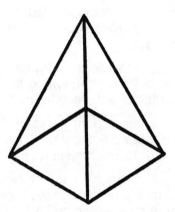

4. Pyrabase—from the base of a four-sided pyramid

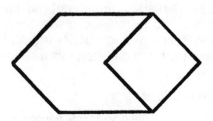

5. Hexabiside—from two sides of a hexagon

8.08 Light Up Your Life

One way to prompt ideas for this exercise is to first make a list of all the relevant characteristics of a light bulb—bulb-shaped, glass, screw action, uses electricity, replaceable, vacuum inside, filament element, breakable, bright, easily turned on and off, emits light beams, glows, etc. Such a list is also likely to help you break away from any constraints you might impose on yourself about a light bulb and, consequently, will result in more creative solutions.

Here are a few possible solutions for each object:

bookcase: sliding glass doors, lighted shelves, electrically opened doors, easily broken down and reassembled, vacuum to keep dust out

mailbox: transparent to see mail, lights up when mail arrives, doubles as a lamp post, spring to automatically reclose mailbox door, box unscrews from post to stop delivery

calculator: screws into a pen, glows in the dark, can be used to activate other electrical devices, disposable calculators, projects data on a wall screen

broom: handle unscrews for easy storage, doubles as a flashlight, shaking the broom makes it glow so it can be used as a toy space sword, shine light through bristles for sweeping in dark corners, top of handle screws into a fixture for easy hanging when not in use

lawn mower: vacuum pickup of grass clippings, inexpensive, replaceable blade, transparent gas tank to tell when empty, filament line to replace blade, light for dawn and dusk mowing, filament track underground to guide mowing, automatically turns off when hits a solid object

8.09 Word to Word

Bit-Ply	Plywood formed into parquet patterns.
Rat-Tulip	A new breed of tulip that "eats" household flies.

Brat-Lip	A pliable cup lip for children to teethe on.
Tab-Tip	A tab pull for soda cans with a tip that is convenient to pull, eliminating injured fingernails.
At-Pit	Name for a barbecue restaurant.
It-Plum	New fruit dessert.
Rib-Put	Device to secure injured ribs.
Bat-My	New children's baseball game that can be played by one child alone.
Bib-Mill	A bib to collect grounds from a coffee mill.
Bait-Pill	New bait form for fishing.
Bra-Pull	A quick-release brassiere.

8.10 Name That Exercise

Chapter 4

Current Name	*Possible New Name*
Goal Visualization	Seeing Ahead
How Much Are You Worth?	Dollars and Sense
Think About It	Creative Living
Early Bird	Rise to the Occasion
Imagine That	Picture Yourself
Bunny Hop	Splitting Hares
Problem Detective	Creative Divorce
Quadruple D	All in the Family
Nitty Gritty	Getting to It
What Problem?	Look It Over

Chapter 5

Current Name	*Possible New Name*
Your Room	Know Your Space
The Picnic	Eating Out
Touch It	In a Bag
I Hear Ya	Sound It Out
Sensory Stretch	Out to Sense
Be a Banana	Dining With the Monkeys

Mowing Along	Can You Cut It?
Goodness Sakes	A Positive Eye
Cube Imagery	Shape Sorter
Orange Elephant	Color Me Orange

Chapter 6

Current Name	*Possible New Name*
Square Off	Lines Galore
Don't Fence Me In	Hold Off
Create a Viewpoint	Silly Patterns
Switch Around	Rotating Dots
Symbol Relatives	What Is That?
Spy Telegrams	Secret Messages
Breakdown	Tear It Apart
Take a Stand	Look But Don't Touch
Take It Off	A Jug of Wine and ...
Just Like That	Almost the Same
SDRAWKCAB	Turnaround
Would You Believe?	Stretch 'n' Solve
Fantasyland	Daydreams
Silly Inventions	Make It Weird
Just Suppose	Design a House

Chapter 7

Current Name	*Possible New Name*
Brain Gusher	Mind Poppers
Pre-fix It	But First ...
Letter Hunt	Lost Letters
Underweight	Taking It Lightly
Word Chains	Linking Words
Sniff Out	Bottle It
Word Relatives	Something Like It
Gar·bägé	Stinking Ideas
Go to Class	Grouping Around
Don't Forget	Try to Recall
Column Relatives	Force It
Just Alike, Only Different	Common Grounds
It Came From Beneath the Blot	Blot It Out

What's In a Name

Spy Stories

Bureaucrat's Delight

Storyteller

Chapter 8

Current Name

Possible New Name

Current Name	Possible New Name
Steaming Ideas	What's Bugging You?
Fill Out	Sketch It
Draw-a-Word	Picture Words
Picture That	Sign In
Something New	Break and Change
Grid Lock	Pick an Object, Any Object
Label It	Call It Like It Is
Light Up Your Life	An Illuminating Idea
Word to Word	Backward Inventing
Name That Exercise	Call It Something
The Master	A Crumbling Experience
End It All	Long John Shiver
Nasal Nonsense	A Nose by Any Other Name
Pork Role	Pig Out
Create an Exercise	Starting Over

Chapter 9

Current Name

Possible New Name

Current Name	Possible New Name
Values	It's Worth It
Wired Up	A Wiry Choice
Light the Way	Lamp of Your Life
Category Crunch	Groupies
Weigh In	Car Trouble

Chapter 10

Current Name

Possible New Name

Current Name	Possible New Name
Idea Garden	Dig It
Freeze-Unfreeze	Cold Shoulder
Consultant	Thanks, Uncle Harry
You Can Take This Job and ...	Take Charge
I Scream	Never on Sundae

8.11   The Master

One possible interpretation would involve the "chain of life" concept. That is, small bugs eat crumbs, the small bugs are eaten by bigger bugs, which in turn are eaten by small animals, which are eaten by larger animals, which then are eaten by humans (still larger animals). At the interpersonal or societal levels, for example, the chain of life could be a metaphor for how we all are dependent on one another in some way. Thus, our potential to meet the needs of each other could be viewed as part of the purpose of our existence.

8.12   End It All

For inside the room he saw eight burly-looking men standing around one slender, frightened man who was completely naked. But what was most distinctive about the naked man was the way he appeared to be shivering. His knees were flapping together but his upper body didn't seem to be cold at all.

Quickly scanning the scene, Greg's eyes caught hold of what he had feared most. Over in one corner, neatly hung on a polished wooden hanger, was a pair of white long johns—for the legs only. From the way they were swinging freely on the hanger, Greg surmised that they just had been removed from the man. It was then that he knew. Yes, this is it—the lair of the dreaded Long John Dons, notorious for their savage acts of forced long-john removal in the coldest of weather!

8.13   Nasal Nonsense

...and saw Dr. Septum examining Nurse Spray's nose. They hadn't heard her enter yet, so she was able to overhear a portion of their conversation. From what she could gather, Dr. Septum was fitting Sally for a new nose.

"That feels pretty good, doctor," Sally said as the

doctor adjusted the artificial nose over her own. "Now I'll have a nose just as big as Dr. Snaffle's."

Cora was flabbergasted. She interrupted their conversation and, although startled, they agreed to let Cora examine Sally's new nose. Cora was so impressed that she asked Dr. Septum to fit her with one. Dr. Septum reached into his nose bag and pulled one out, placing it carefully on Cora's nose. At that very moment Cora realized that here was the answer to her problem—right over her very own nose!

8.14 Pork Role

Hog production can be a confusing business, to say the least. In addition to the need for tolerance of continual squealing, there must be an efficient way of processing large numbers of these creatures. One major problem is separating the large from the small pigs for processing. Although it is easy to tell the very large from the very small pig, only a trained porkologist can decide about pigs of moderate size, since regulations require either a large or small size classification.

One company solved this problem by hiring Professor Porcine to advise them. The professor said that the simple solution is often the best. His suggestion was for porkologists to tie a long string to the tail of every small pig, so that when the pigs went to processing, the processors could easily make the necessary distinction.

8.15 Create That Exercise

If you turned to this page expecting to see fourteen more exercises, you'll be disappointed. Do you think I can make up exercises forever?!!! You're the one who's supposed to do the work this time!

All seriousness aside, you may gain more from doing this exercise than from most of the others combined. By having to develop material instead of reacting to it, your understanding of basic creative-thinking principles should increase immensely. There's really no substitute for doing. In addition, this exercise required you to use both sides of your brain ... something we all need a little more practice doing.

When you've finished all of your exercises, rate yourself on your own originality. Use a seven-point scale to describe each of your exercises as being not very original (1) to very original (7). Then try to figure out why you rated the exercises the way you did. If you didn't rate yourself very high, it may be because you have an unrealistic expectation standard. The exercises in this book probably are no better or worse than your own. You are unique and you shouldn't expect to do everything like all the rest of us. If you rated your exercises very high in originality, then you probably should be writing your own book instead of wasting your time reading this one. Or perhaps you have expanded the powers of your creative mind from just doing the other exercises in this book. In either event, it would be time to pat your right brain for a job well done.

If you are especially pleased with any of your exercises, I would be interested in seeing them. Just send them to me in care of the publisher (Prentice-Hall, Inc., Englewood Cliffs, N.J. 07632). If I should ever do another edition of this book I may be able to include some of them in it. You, of course, will be given full credit. I won't be able to return any, so make yourself an extra copy if you wish.

YOU'RE
THE JUDGE

Making decisions is my second most favorite thing to do. My most favorite activity is trying to flush my head down a toilet. I really don't like to make decisions. It is much easier to hope a problem goes away and solves itself or to let someone else do the dirty work of decision making. Of course, I don't want to totally avoid making decisions, especially if there might be something in the outcome for me. But if I could, I generally would prefer to delegate a good number of my decisions to other people—say, a special personal decision-making committee. This way, by the time they got around to making a decision, the original problem might have disappeared.

Unfortunately (at least for me and others with similar feelings), we can't avoid making decisions. They are all around us, continually demanding our attention. As much as we might hope they'll go away, they just don't. To survive, we have to face and deal with decisions every day. So we might as well learn to do the best we can.

In the area of creative problem solving, decision making is one activity that many people frequently overlook. A common assumption is that creativity is limited to generating ideas. However, it is a rare situation in which all ideas produced can be used to solve a problem. There has to be some way of narrowing down the ideas to just one or a few for implementation. Unpleasant though it may be, we do need to consider what factors tend to influence us and what procedures we use in making our decisions.

To do the five exercises in this chapter, you will need to relax your creative brain a bit and switch over a little more to the analytical mode. Don't completely abandon your right brain, however, since you still will need to use it for such activities as generating selection criteria and evaluating the factors and values that influence your final decision. Nevertheless, considerably more logic will be required to complete most of these exercises in contrast to the ones in the previous chapter.

The first exercise is concerned with a general assessment of the personal values you bring to bear in solving problems. The objective is to increase your awareness about these values so that you will be more satisfied with the outcomes of your decisions. The second and third exercises look at more general factors that you might use in making decisions, but they also consider your values as well. The fourth exercise is concerned specifically with narrowing down and combining ideas to make a final choice easier. The last exercise is somewhat quantitative in nature. But don't panic if numbers aren't your strong point. This exercise simply involves use of a systematic technique for selecting from among a few equally attractive alternatives. You can use it for such decisions as buying a house or a car, but don't bother with it if the hardest decision you ever have to make is choosing between a green or blue outfit to wear to work.

If you had trouble suspending judgment while doing

the other exercises, then you should thrive on this chapter. Let your critical mind go, but don't forget that many "bad" ideas sometimes can be improved on and transformed into "good" ideas. A critical mind is fine when it is used properly, but it also needs to be an open mind.

9.01   Values

The importance of values in decision making can't be minimized. Values affect the way we perceive problem situations and, perhaps most importantly, guide us in making choices. Too often, however, many of us make decisions without being fully aware of what specific values have influenced us. If we could increase awareness about our own personal values, then we might be more satisfied with the outcomes of our decisions.

For this exercise, you are to try and identify which values guided you in making some important decision in the past. First, think of some of the major decisions you made within the last couple of years, e.g., a career choice, getting married, deciding to have children, a major financial commitment, etc. Select one of these decisions and list at least ten values that influenced your choice in some way. Then rank these values in terms of how much they influenced your final decision. List the most influential value first, the second most influential value second, and so forth until you have ranked all of the values you considered.

In case you have trouble thinking of different types of values, some examples are: power, prestige, security, freedom, and conformity. However, don't feel restricted to just these and similar types of values. Include whatever you believe influenced your choice.

9.02   Wired Up

Assume that you are the president of a company that manufactures wire coat hangers. Business has been so good lately that you decide to branch out and seek new markets for your product. After conducting a brainstorming meeting with your staff, you are left with a list of the twenty-five ideas presented below.

Your task is to select five of these ideas for serious consideration as new product lines. When making your choices, write down the factors that influenced you, paying particular attention to *why* they influenced you.

1. hose clamps
2. tie-downs for truck tarps
3. key rings
4. edging for shrubbery
5. puzzle games
6. plant hangers
7. barbecue skewers
8. cooking grills
9. darts
10. pipe cleaners
11. bucket handles
12. picture hangers
13. mousetraps
14. hole punchers
15. back scratchers
16. tie racks
17. letters for signs
18. small bird and animal cages
19. springs
20. shower-curtain rings
21. melt and use as fishing weights
22. trellis for climbing plants
23. axles for toy cars
24. Christmas wreaths
25. sculptures

9.03 Light the Way

It often is difficult to make a decision when we have several alternatives from which to choose. Furthermore, two people can vary considerably in the factors they use in making a decision. Some people might be influenced by one particular aspect of an alternative, some might be influenced by an overall impression, and others might make full use of all available information to make a choice.

This exercise is designed to help you assess how you go about making decisions when confronted with four different alternatives. To receive the most benefit from this exercise, try to be aware of all the factors that influence your choice. The best way to do this is to write down each factor as you consider it. Try to be as specific as possible.

Four designs for a table lamp are shown in Figure 9.1. Which design do you like best? Which design do you like least? To make your decision, develop separate lists of the things you like and dislike about each lamp.

Figure 9.1 Proposed Designs for a Tablelamp

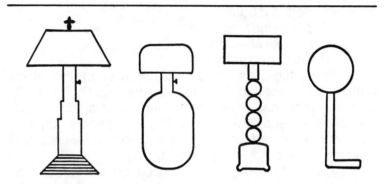

9.04   Category Crunch

When a large number of possible problem solutions has been generated, it can be difficult to select only one or two to implement. This is especially true when there are several equally attractive alternatives. In this situation, the time or other resources needed to implement more than one or two possible solutions isn't always available.

One way out of this dilemma is to combine and modify several ideas to produce just one or two final solutions. This is done by clustering similar ideas into categories and then modifying or combining two or more ideas within the categories to produce one workable idea. You then can work with successively more narrow categories until only three or four remain. Thus, you might initially start with ten or more categories and then gradually reduce these in number by combining some of them into broader categories.

Suppose, for example, that you had generated different uses for a one-gallon plastic milk container. Among the ideas you might generate are:

1. funnel
2. flowerpot
3. storage for emergency water supply
4. disposing of used engine oil
5. party hat
6. bird feeder
7. flotation buoy
8. packaging material
9. toys for children
10. small-parts storage

These ten uses could be categorized in three ways (among other possibilities): (1) as a container (2, 3, 4, 6, 10), (2) as a functional device other than a container (1, 7, 8), and (3) as a decorative item (5, 9). These three categories then might be reduced to just two: (1) containers and functional devices and (2) decorative items.

The number of items could be further reduced by combining items within categories. Thus, a funnel and small-parts storage might suggest a funnel-type device for holding screws—whenever you need a screw you tap the device and a screw falls out.

To try your hand at this process, combine and modify the following solutions for a problem on how to obtain funds for a nonprofit preschool center:

1. have a telethon
2. have an auction
3. start a magazine
4. get company sponsors
5. solicit contributions from community "fat cats"
6. have a fund-raising carnival
7. baby-sit for a professional fund-raising organization in exchange for their services
8. have children collect donations door to door
9. have a concert
10. seek a federal grant
11. write a book
12. have a bake sale
13. take care of pets for a fee

14. make and sell ice cream
15. get a university film department to produce a fund-raising film to show on TV and to various community groups
16. solicit funds from rich relatives
17. make and sell toys
18. get free public-service announcements on TV and radio
19. publish a newsletter
20. have a raffle

9.05   Weigh-In

When most of us make decisions about everyday affairs, we use relatively simple guidelines to help us choose. For example, we might say, "Product A costs less than products B and C. Therefore, I will buy product A." When we make such decisions, we may be unaware of other factors we unconsciously considered. Or at least we don't pay as much attention to them as we do to an item's cost. Normally, such a procedure results in a satisfactory decision.

There are times, however, when a more structured and systematic procedure might be more useful and lead to higher-quality decisions. Typically, such times involve high-cost decisions in terms of the resources involved. That is, it may be difficult to obtain all the information needed; the information may be available but difficult to interpret or organize; or failure to make a high-quality decision may result in serious consequences. When a decision is important, a systematic way of approaching it can make the difference between success and failure.

This exercise provides practice in choosing from among three high-cost alternatives. It is classified as a high-cost situation because of the financial commitment involved on the part of the decision makers.

Assume that you have spent the entire day trudging around town in search of a replacement for the six-year-old family wagon, the same car that failed to start on the morning your wife was about to give birth to your last child. The same car that decided to take a vacation in the airport parking lot when you returned from yours.

The children are now screaming and your spouse's back is acting up again. Luckily, you have narrowed your choice to three cars. Make your final choice using the following procedure:

1. List all the factors that will influence your decision.
2. Rate each factor on a one- to five-point scale in terms of its importance to you (1 = not very important; 5 = very important). This is the importance rating.
3. Think of three cars you actually would consider buying.
4. Rate each of these cars (1 = not at all; 5 = completely) in terms of how well they meet the importance ratings you established in Step 2. This is the satisfaction rating.
5. Multiply each importance rating times each satisfaction rating for the three cars. For example, if you rated price 5 on importance and gave car A a 3 on this factor, you would multiply 3 times 5 to get 15.
6. Add up the products (obtained from multiplying) for each car and make your decision.

If you have trouble following these directions, study the example shown in Table 9.1. Then try to develop your own decision chart.

Table 9.1   *Decision Chart for Selecting a Car*

Satisfaction	Importance	Car A		Car B		Car C	
1. Price	5	3	15	5	25	1	5
2. Gas mileage	5	4	20	3	15	2	10
3. Color	3	5	15	1	3	5	15
4. Dealer service	4	4	16	5	20	5	20
5. Handling and comfort	4	4	16	3	12	5	20
6. Repair record	5	4	20	5	25	4	20
7. Seating capacity	5	3	15	2	10	5	25
8. Ease of servicing	3	5	15	2	6	3	9
9. Trade-in value	2	5	10	2	4	3	6
10. Styling	4	5	20	3	12	5	20
			162		132		150

Based on the final ratings, car A would be selected over cars B and C.

COMMENTS AND SAMPLE ANSWERS

9.01   Values

Values for a career decision might be ranked as follows, but obviously will vary from person to person:

1. self-development
2. security
3. sense of accomplishment
4. advancement
5. self-esteem
6. independence
7. happiness
8. competence
9. power
10. prestige

The next time you have to make an important decision, try listing the values that come into play and order them as you did for this exercise. See if you can use this ranking to help you make your choice. Then, sometime after you have made a decision, assess your overall satisfaction with it. If you were aware of all the values involved in your decision, you should be much happier with the outcome (assuming, of course, you had a certain degree of freedom in making your decision).

9.02   Wired Up

Regardless of which products you selected, some of the factors that influenced you may be specific just to you, while others may be more general. For example, you might have considered such specific factors as avoiding sharp bends that could crack the paint, similarity to the actual item (e.g., a coat-hanger wire looks more like shrubbery edging than it does like most auto-hose clamps), and degree of innovativeness. More general factors would include such things as ease of assembly, cost, likely market, and compatibility with existing channels of distribution. The reasons these factors influenced you probably say something about your values as well as any knowledge you might have about developing and marketing new products.

9.03 Light the Way

This exercise is similar to the other exercises in this chapter in that you are required to assess your personal values in making a choice, only this time you were asked to focus on your specific likes and dislikes. In addition, the objects of your choice involve values different from some of those you may have considered in the previous exercises. The values in this exercise were of a more aesthetic nature, and you were required to respond to visual shapes rather than more abstract concepts.

In making your judgments, you might have begun with some general categories such as traditional, modern, or antique. These simply are indicators of your style preferences for such items. The reasons you have such preferences are, of course, difficult to determine. However, many of us are influenced in such matters by our background experiences, particularly in regard to the influences of significant others in our lives. Can you think of any people who may have influenced you in such a manner?

In evaluating your experience with this exercise, you also might ask yourself such questions as: Did your likes and dislikes tend to fall into similar categories? How did you process the information you used to make a final choice? Did you use a sequential procedure or did you tend to skip around a lot? Did you put more weight on overall appearance or were you influenced more by one particular aspect, such as a shade or base?

When answering these questions, ask yourself why you thought the way you did. Just as awareness of a problem is important when you begin trying to solve it, so is awareness of why you make the decisions you do.

9.04   Category Crunch

From the list of twenty ideas, the following are representative of the types of groups that might be developed initially:

Grouping:	Idea Number:
Publications	3, 11, 19
Media	1, 15, 18
Manufacturing	14, 17
Services	7, 13
Solicit funds	4, 5, 8, 10, 16
Sponsor one-time activities	2, 6, 9, 12, 20

These categories then might be combined as follows:

Grouping:	Idea Number:
Publications	3, 11, 19
Products and services	7, 13, 14, 17
Solicitations and sponsored activities	1, 2, 4, 5, 6, 8, 9, 10, 12, 15, 16, 18, 20

Of course, not all ideas will lend themselves to additional groupings; the decision to do so will depend on the type and number of ideas.

Assuming that some form of categorization is possible, however, the next step is to determine if any ideas might be combined to produce new solutions. In the example above, the ideas for a telethon, auction, fat-cat contributions, and seeking a federal grant could be combined to suggest a new approach. For instance, federal funds might be sought to sponsor a series of monthly educational TV programs that would attract viewers by holding a phone-in auction of items donated by community fat cats. The remainder of the program then would be devoted to discussing educational needs of young children and requesting donations.

9.05   *Weigh-In*

Even after going through all the steps involved in making a decision using this procedure, you may decide that you don't want to abide by the final outcome. Instead, your gut instinct may be to go with car C, for example. If you do make such a decision, go back over each of the ratings before you commit yourself. See if there are any ratings you would change. Then try to think of any other factors you may have left out when you originally developed your list. A common error is to reject the final rating without being aware of the basis for such a decision. Reviewing the factor list and the ratings can help insure that this error does not occur. Of course, it's your money, and if you will feel better going by instinct, then spend away!

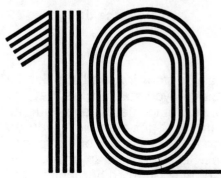

AVOIDING
SURPRISES

Murphy's Law states, If anything can go wrong, it will. Try dropping a piece of jelly toast on your kitchen floor. Which side usually lands where your young daughter just lost her breakfast? Or, go on a trip feeling confident and proud that you finally remembered to bring along your toothbrush. Now where was it you put the toothpaste?

Although we may try to anticipate problems, we're not always successful. There usually is some unanticipated event that seems to develop at the last minute. This is especially true when trying to implement relatively complex projects. The first launching of the space shuttle is a perfect example. Without detracting from the eventual magnificence of this achievement, the computer malfunction that occurred during the final stages of the countdown theoretically could have been avoided. However, humans were involved, and we haven't all reached a state of perfection yet (I know a few individuals who would have me believe otherwise about themselves).

It should be self-evident that the best ideas in the world will be of little value unless they can be implemented with some likelihood of success. However, we often invest so much effort in trying to solve a problem that we may ease up a bit when the time comes to apply our solution. It is so much easier just to go ahead and do something than to spend time in thinking through how to do it. As a result, planning and implementation seem to be two very neglected elements of the creative problem-solving process.

Although there is little doubt that these two elements are important, it can be difficult to develop the motivation or the resources needed to give them the attention they deserve. Unfortunately, we can't find motivation in a book or buy it in a store. We can, however, practice using some exercises and methods that might increase our awareness about the need for more planning and anticipating in creative problem solving. Five exercises for just that purpose are included in this chapter.

The first exercise looks at the need to develop a creative climate to gain acceptance of your ideas; the second allows you to evaluate your persuasive and analytical powers; the third involves you in assessing your personal strengths relevant to implementing ideas; the fourth requires you to systematically anticipate some potential implementation problems; and the fifth requires you to develop an implementation planning diagram.

Above all, these last five exercises force you to make full use of both sides of your brain. To do otherwise at this point in the process could lead to a less-than-satisfactory outcome. If you are too analytical at this stage, you may overlook many potential problems and creative ways of overcoming them; if you are too creative, then you may have trouble developing a systematic procedure that will allow your ideas to be implemented. Your goal should be to integrate the functioning of both of your brain hemispheres.

10.01   Idea Garden

Because so many things can go wrong when attempting to implement an idea, it is important that all possible contingencies be considered. However, there is one aspect of implementation that frequently is overlooked: the need for the right kind of creative climate. Unless the environment is receptive, your idea will stand little chance of surviving and achieving the objectives you set for it. Thus, you must consider what, if anything, needs changing before you can put your idea to work.

Just as a garden cannot be planted without some preliminary work, so must you prepare the "soil" for your ideas to grow. For example, in planting a garden you will need to decide what to plant, check the soil to determine if it contains the essential nutrients, plow the earth to break any resistance that the seedlings might encounter, add fertilizer, plant the seeds, and then water on a regular basis.

Using this analogy of a garden, describe the steps you might take to develop a creative climate to ask your boss for a raise.

10.02   Freeze-Unfreeze

The value of any creative idea really can't be measured until it gains acceptance from the potential users. This basic fact of creativity is especially true in such areas as new-product development, where only a very small percentage of proposed ideas actually ever reaches the commercialization stage. It is also true, however, for any other area of life in which one person is trying to persuade another about the merits of a particular idea.

The key to gaining acceptance of an idea usually lies with the persuasive powers of the idea originator or those responsible for putting the idea into action. The process involved in persuading others about the value of and need for an idea can be made more manageable if a little time is spent anticipating possible objections and analyzing likely benefits. By carefully weighing in advance the factors likely to be judged in assessing the worth of an idea, the potential for eventual acceptance can be greatly enhanced. However, any objections first must be unfrozen in order to gain any measure of acceptance.

This exercise will give you a chance to test your persuasive and analytical powers on a new product recently introduced into the market. The product is known as Frig-I-Door; it is manufactured by the BSL Corporation. Frig-I-Doors are simply curtains of heavy clear-plastic strips that are hung across frozen-food cases (using Velcro fasteners) in supermarkets to keep cold air in and hot air out. Customers make their selections by reaching between the strips. A four-foot section of the strips costs about ninety dollars.

Assume that you are involved in marketing this product. What are the primary benefits of this product that could be used to sell it to supermarket officials? What objections to the product would you anticipate and how could you counter them?

10.03   Consultant

Would you like to be on your own with no one to tell you what to do? Why not become a consultant? You'll have your own hours, and the sky is the limit in terms of how much money you can make. Well, why not? What? You also like to eat and have a house to live in? Don't let those little details bother you. Assume that rich old Uncle Harry has agreed to bankroll your attempt to be a consultant so that your own risk is minimal. So go right ahead and begin planning. The following questions and guidelines might be helpful.

1. Think of all your major strengths and skills.
2. Which one could you turn into a profitable service to others? How do you know?
3. Develop a name for your service.
4. How much initial capital will you need?

5. Who will be your market and how will you reach them?
6. Who is your competition?
7. Develop a small brochure in which you describe your services.

10.04   You Can Take This Job and . . .

OK. That's the last time you'll sit there and take it while your boss reams you out for not doing things his way. You've had it; you decide to quit. You feel a lot better, but what are you going to do now? Aha! Become your own boss and you won't have to take any more guff. All right, if you think it's so easy, go ahead. You're the boss. Start your own business, using the following guidelines and questions:

1. What kind of business would be best for you? Why?
2. What will you call your company?
3. What will be your market? Who is the competition?
4. Where should you locate?
5. Develop an organizational chart.
6. Define your short- and long-term goals.
7. Should you incorporate? If so, what would be the best way?
8. How should you advertise and market your product or service?
9. How many employees will you need?

After dealing with these issues and any others you can think of, try to generate a list of all possible factors that could go wrong (this is known as negative creativity or reverse brainstorming). For example, suppose that you decide to make hula hoops and the market for this product declines after six months. What will you do with your excess inventory? Will it put you out of business, or will you be able to adapt and develop a new product or marketing strategy?

Once you have developed your negative-creativity list, you should go back over your original plan and examine it to see if you might need to change anything. If you are satisfied that you haven't left out anything and don't need to make any changes, develop a specific action (preventive action) to counter each negative consequence. For those negative consequences that could put you out of business, develop back-up or contingency plans. Then leave this exercise and go do something else. Stay away for at least an hour. When you return, review the entire plan again. Are you able to find something you overlooked the first time? If so, you are doing a pretty good job of making sure that you won't receive an unexpected and disastrous surprise.

10.05   I Scream

Most of the activities we engage in are based on some sort of plan. This plan may be very carefully thought out in advance, or it may be put into action without much advance thought, relying instead on past experience. Activities we are used to doing require little in the way of planning. However, whenever we must implement some new activity (especially one of some importance to ourselves or others) it is often necessary to develop some form of plan.

The plans we develop for new activities can be extremely simple or complex, ranging from a brief checklist of things to do to highly complex flow charts that require computers to monitor and control their implementation. Somewhere in between these two extremes lies an implementation method known as planning diagrams.

Planning diagrams are relatively simple flow charts that show what needs to be done and how it should be done. The core of these diagrams consists of various decision points that are used to guide all subsequent activities. Thus, a planning diagram is really just a network of activities and decision points. A certain skill, however, can be required in determining what activities to include and how they should be related.

To illustrate, consider the task of brushing your teeth.

A portion of a planning diagram that could be used to guide the actions required is shown in Figure 10.1.

Try your hand at developing a planning diagram for constructing an ice cream sundae. The sundae is to be made of vanilla ice cream, chocolate syrup, and nuts. It is to be eaten in a bowl with a spoon.

Figure 10.1 Partial Planning Diagram for Toothbrushing

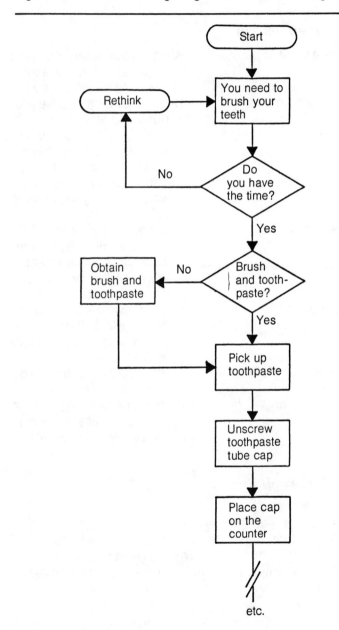

COMMENTS AND SAMPLE ANSWERS

10.01 Idea Garden

1. Decide what to plant	Weigh your strengths and weaknesses; decide what needs to be emphasized.
2. Check the soil	Determine how receptive your boss is to employees asking for raises; determine what approach is likely to produce the most favorable response; determine which times your boss is in the best mood.
3. Plow the earth	Test your boss's receptivity by generally discussing your work performance; point out the contributions you have made.
4. Add fertilizer	Have co-workers or other persons in authority mention your qualifications to your boss.
5. Plant the seeds	Mention that you think you deserve a raise.
6. Water regularly	If not immediately given the raise, periodically mention the subject to your boss.

10.02 Freeze-Unfreeze

Product Benefits
1. Decreased energy costs.
2. Cooler temperatures mean longer shelf life.
3. Hot weather shutdowns will be minimized.
4. Adjacent aisles are kept warmer, thus making

shopping more comfortable for the shopper, especially during the winter.

5. Easy to clean.
6. Possibly lower costs to consumer due to reduced energy costs.

Objections	*Countering Comments*
1. Initial cost. A thirty-six-foot section on a case will cost about eight hundred dollars.	Research has shown that energy costs will drop 20 to 30 percent, thus offsetting the initial investment in a short period of time.
2. Appearance detracts from attractive food display.	Will be partially offset by increased customer comfort during cold weather and perhaps lower food costs.
3. Strips would make re-shelving difficult.	Velcro fasteners make it easy to peel away the screens to restock food items.

In addition, a trial period could be offered: If energy costs are not substantially reduced, the product could be returned for a partial refund.

10.03 Consultant

Perhaps the most important activity in this exercise is the list of your strengths and weaknesses. This kind of awareness is necessary for implementing any type of idea. You must know when you are capable of competently and effectively carrying out some activity, and when you must seek assistance. For instance, you may think you know how to develop a brochure to market your services, but find out that few people are attracted by it or understand exactly what services you are offering.

Confidence in yourself is very important when you

are planning any sort of activity. However, you just can't beat plain old self-awareness when it comes to putting an idea into practice.

10.04   You Can Take This Job and . . .

This exercise is specifically designed to provide you with practice in anticipating potential implementation problems and in developing means to circumvent these problems.

A corollary to Murphy's Law states that if you think of four things that could go wrong and develop ways to get around them, then a fifth thing promptly will develop. Although this may be true, the more anticipating you do, the fewer problems you will have to deal with when trying to implement your ideas.

Suppose that you decided to develop a mail-order business to sell gold-plated toothpicks. One way you could have dealt with any potential problems during the planning phase would have been to use a chart listing possible problems and actions that could be taken in case something goes wrong. Such a chart is shown in Table 10.1, using both preventive and contingency actions.

Table 10.1   Analysis of Potential Problems for a Toothpick Business

Potential Problems	Preventive Actions	Contingency Plans
1. Wood in short supply	Substitute plastic	Raise prices
2. Gold in short supply	Substitute silver	Raise prices; use gold paint
3. Cost of wood too high	Raise prices	Substitute plastic
4. Cost of gold too high	Raise prices	Sell conventional toothpicks
5. Not enough customers	Offer discounts	Hire ad agency
6. Toothpicks break when first used	Use quality control	

7. Competition too   Lower prices   Use deluxe pack-
   tough   aging; aim for
                                          exclusive buyers
8. Cost of factory   Begin production
   space too high   at home
9. No workers in-   Offer profit sharing   Use relatives
   terested in work-
   ing for you

Of course, such a chart will be only as good as the information it contains. If you are not thorough in constructing your chart, then you may develop a false sense of security. Just making a chart is not enough—you must continually review it to make sure you haven't left anything out.

10.05   *I Scream*

The diagram in Figure 10.2 illustrates only one of many different possibilities. Your diagram may be longer or shorter, depending on how much detail you included. It is probably better, however, to include too much detail rather than too little. One way to be more inclusive in your description is to patiently visualize yourself completing all the actions required. Better yet, actually make a sundae and then write down exactly what you did at different stages of the process. (Most of us are surprised at how little attention we pay to how we perform a relatively familiar activity.)

While planning diagrams are not needed for mundane types of activities, they often can make the difference between implementation success or failure in more important types of projects.

Figure 10.2 Planning Diagram for an Ice Cream Sundae

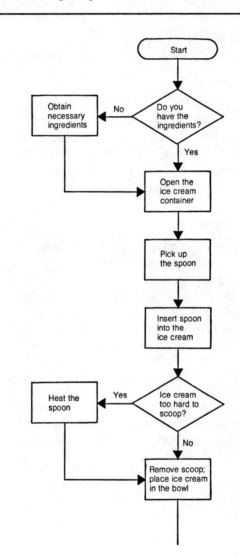

Figure 10.2 Planning Diagram for an Ice Cream Sundae (cont'd.)

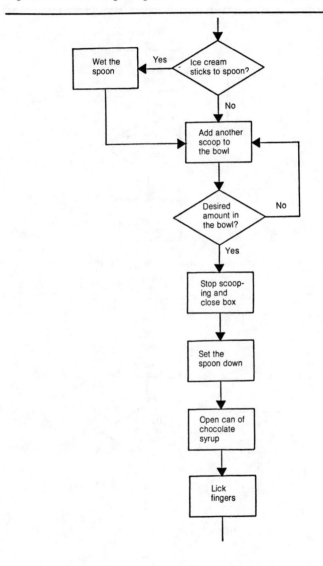

Figure 10.2 Planning Diagram for an Ice Cream Sundae (cont'd.)

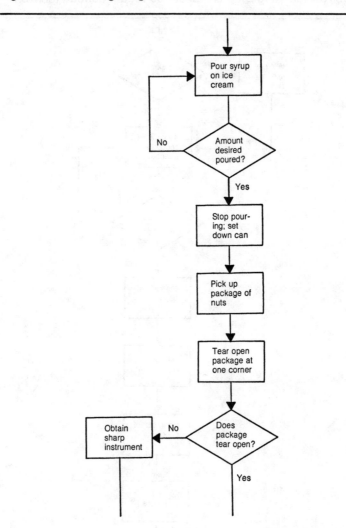

Figure 10.2 Planning Diagram for an Ice Cream Sundae (cont'd.)

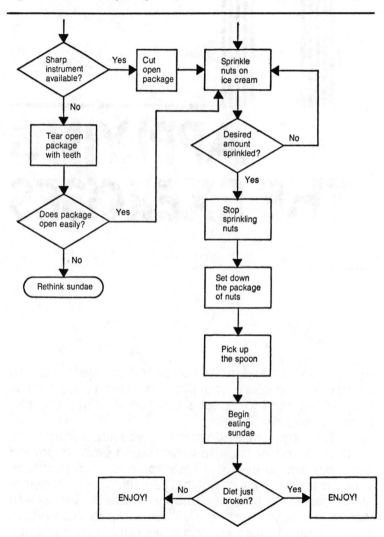

11

APPLYING THE EXERCISES

By now you should have completed the warm-up and intermediate phases of your program at least once. Unless you feel the need to repeat any of the exercises, you can begin the applied phase.

This phase is designed to help you further internalize some of the major creative-thinking and problem-solving concepts, and to help you seek some form of closure to your program. It is important that you begin to pull together all the conscious and even unconscious experiences and learnings that you have gone through up to this point in your program. Unless you can make right-brain thinking a part of your natural thinking processes, you will find that your left brain will easily regain control. And the best way to begin internalizing your newly acquired skills is to apply what you have learned.

As mentioned in Chapter 3, the third phase of your program involves two sets of applied activities. The first activity presents you with a hypothetical problem to work on, using your learnings from the previous phases. The purpose of this activity is to get you thinking about how right-brain processes might help you solve the problem presented. The second activity is similar to the first except that it is a personal problem of your own choosing. While this problem also will require you to practice your right-brain thinking skills, it differs from the first in one important respect: You have "ownership" of this problem. Because of this ownership, your motivation to solve it should be much greater than in the case of the first problem.

Although it is always nice to work on problems with which we can identify, this is not the primary reason for doing so. By being motivated, your problem-solving skills should be heightened to the extent that the overall experience will have more meaning and will be retained or internalized by you to a much greater extent than had you just worked on a problem with little meaning to you. After all, one of your ultimate objectives in completing this program should be to become a better creative thinker. And you can't expect to be a creative thinker unless you are able to think creatively just as routinely as you probably think analytically.

USING A PROBLEM-SOLVING PROCESS

It should be fairly clear to you by now that a major emphasis throughout this book has been on creative thinking as a tool for problem solving. And, as mentioned in the first chapter, the emphasis has been on solving unstructured types of problems—those in which no clear-cut solutions are available. Besides any personal growth benefits you might reap from becoming more creative, the primary benefit to you will be in helping you to become a more effective problem solver. If you think more creatively, you will be able to approach unstructured problems with more confidence and with a greater probability of solving them.

Becoming a more effective problem solver requires some knowledge of the basic problem-solving process. Up to this point I have made little mention about problem solving as a process. I only have made indirect references to it when discussing some principle or concept of creative thinking. You might even say I have neglected this important topic. Well, I have, and the neglect has been intentional.

Problem solving generally is discussed in a strictly left-brain manner. A linear model is presented and then described in terms of the sequential activities required to proceed through each of the stages. Because most people are used to such a left-brained presentation, it can't be criticized in that respect. There has to be some way of communicating information about processes, and a sequential approach to problem solving is one with which most people probably can relate easily. I have used such a presentation myself and probably will continue to do so in those instances in which it seems to be the most appropriate means of communicating my thoughts.

I have intentionally avoided presenting a problem-solving model at the beginning of this book even though it has been a recurrent theme throughout. Although problem solving is integrally related to creative thinking, the emphasis in this book on right-brain thinking led me to defer discussing problem solving until you had progressed through the exercises.

Since the exercises themselves were roughly organized into major problem-solving stages, my hope was that you would learn about many of the activities involved in the creative problem-solving process as you experienced the exercises. For example, when you were doing the exercises in Chapter 4, you were practicing problem preparation and gathering facts about yourself and problems; in Chapter 5 you were experiencing awareness of your different senses and how they can aid you in analyzing problems and generating ideas; in Chapters 6, 7, and 8 you were practicing some of the skills needed to generate ideas: flexibility, fluency, and originality; in Chapter 9 you were looking at how you might evaluate and select ideas; and in Chapter 10 you were practicing gaining acceptance for your ideas and anticipating idea-implementation problems.

All these different activities are involved, in one form or another, with what generally is considered to be the standard creative problem-solving process. An example of this process can be easily depicted as shown in Figure 11.1. Although this model may include fewer or more stages than other similar models, it is fairly typical in the nature of the activities included. Note that it also is a prescriptive model rather than a descriptive model. That is, it shows what *should* occur during the process and not what actually *does* occur.

As usually conceived, the process begins with identification of a problem situation. This is followed by a search for information about the problem to help clarify it. Using this information, a definition of the problem is developed and used as the basis for generating possible solutions. This stage is critical to the entire process since the initial definition will determine the nature of most subsequent activities. After possible solutions have been generated, they must be evaluated, using criteria that will conform to any constraints on the problem, and a solution (or solutions) must be selected. Actions then are taken to gain acceptance for the solution—to smooth the way for its implementation. Finally, the solution is implemented and followed up and monitored in the last stage to insure that it will achieve its objectives.

In Figure 11.1, I also have included various feedback loops to signify that adjustments may have to be made during the course of the process. For instance, new information might become available during the selection stage that could alter the selection of one solution over another. And, after a solution has been implemented, it may

Figure 11.1 Example of a Standard Creative Problem Solving Process

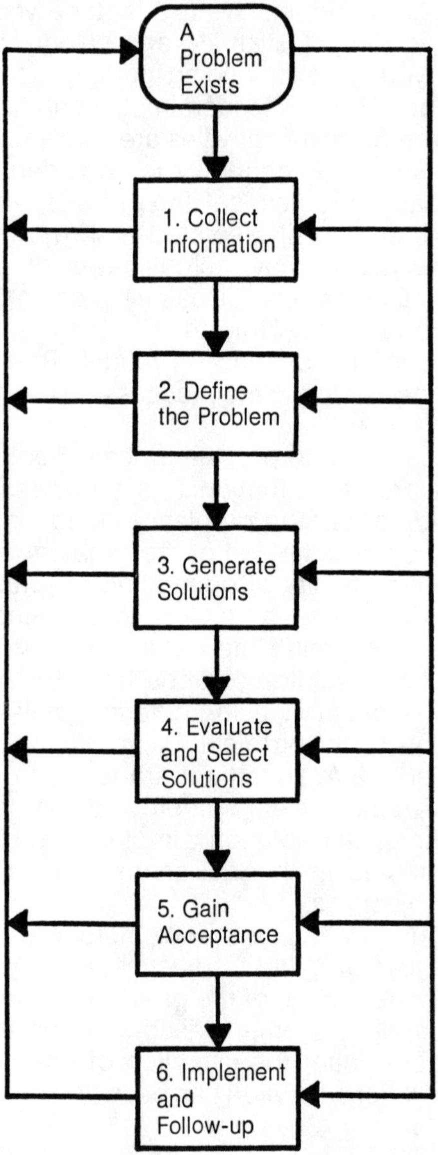

create new problems that could necessitate beginning the process over again. Note that this model is essentially a closed-loop model.

All of this is very rational and logical. The model implies that all of the different stages are relatively clear-cut and, if followed correctly, will lead to a successful solution. However, most of us seldom use such a model to solve our problems, nor should we use it all the time. There are many situations in which muddling through can be just as effective. Nevertheless, whenever there are high costs associated with not solving a problem, we would be wise to adopt a more systematic approach.

The approach that we adopt, however, need not be as structured as that shown in Figure 11.1. The approach we use should be one that we can conceptualize easily and with which we can identify easily. We need to start thinking of the creative problem-solving process in terms of our own right brains. That is, how can we personally visualize this set of ongoing activities that will take us from a problem "mess" to some sort of satisfactory solution?

My personal attempt at such a visualization is shown in Figure 11.2. To me, this type of conceptualization is much more logical than the standard model. The numbers represent the same activities as represented in Figure 11.1, but in this case there is no prescribed sequence. In fact, several different solution paths are represented in the figure.

After being confronted with the initial mess, you might proceed in any direction, since the numbers represent points in undefined space. The direction followed will be based on intuition and logic. You could proceed in a linear fashion or skip from one stage to another. This is not to say, however, that there is or should be complete chaos to the process. Some type of format has to be followed in order to make progress toward the goal of resolving the problem mess. You have to experience some forward movement, but it doesn't have to be orderly or strictly sequential. Thus, the path you choose in Figure 11.2 probably will vary for

Figure 11.2 Example of a Modified Creative Problem Solving Process

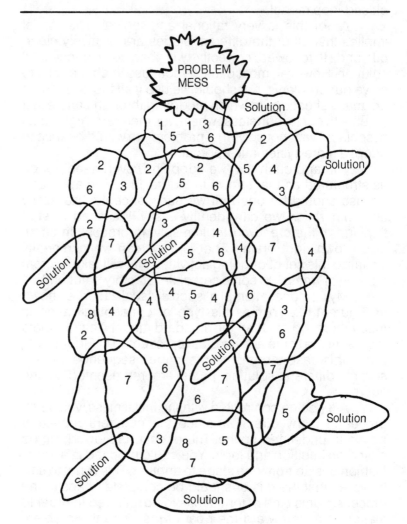

each problem. Also note that you might solve the problem at any time. The outcome doesn't have to occur at the end of some linear process. Circumstances may be such that things just fall into place and the problem is solved.

If you think about it, this is what usually happens when most of us deal with unstructured problems. However, too often we succumb to our left brains and try to maintain a logical, sequential procedure. Then, when this method fails to work, we may revert to a completely right-brain approach, but end up making little progress. What I am suggesting is that we need to capitalize on the strengths of both our hemispheres when we use the creative problem-solving approach. We need to recognize the need for different activities, but we shouldn't become overly concerned about performing these activities in any prescribed sequence. That is, we need to be more holistic and concerned about relationships than about whether a specific set of activities has been correctly carried out at the correct time.

To apply this type of thinking, you should consider what approach will be best for you to use in working on the hypothetical and personal problems. In order to retain some consistency with the presentation format of the exercises, I suggest that you think in terms of the following general stages: 1) problem preparation and information collecting, 2) problem awareness and definition development, 3) testing problem assumptions and constraints, 4) solution generation, 5) solution refinement, 6) solution evaluation and selection, and 7) implementation planning. Of course, you shouldn't feel that you have to be locked into these particular stages. Feel free to vary the procedure you use as long as you seem to be making progress toward a solution. At a minimum, you should try to separate your efforts into broad stages of: 1) analyzing the problem, 2) generating ideas, 3) evaluating and selecting ideas, and 4) planning implementation. You might skip around a little between these four areas, but you should strive for forward progression through them. As mentioned, you do need to have some degree of goal orientation, even though it may be slightly fuzzy at the outset.

PROBLEM NUMBER ONE

Here's the hypothetical problem for you to use in applying your learnings from the exercises:

> Assume that you are the president of a large chain of department stores. In recent years, several of the stores have been plagued by increasing losses due to shoplifting. In what ways might you reduce shoplifting in these stores?

Allow yourself two weeks to work on this problem, devoting at least twenty minutes per day to it. After you have worked through the entire process, compare your responses with the partially worked-out example at the end of the chapter. You might find that some of the sample responses will suggest new ways of approaching the problem or new solutions. If you are stimulated by the example, go ahead and make any changes you wish to your own responses. Be careful, however, that you don't use the example as the "correct" approach or as your primary standard of comparison. The responses in the example are only representative of the types of responses that might be used. They definitely are not exhaustive, nor do they represent the only way the problem can be approached.

You can use the following questions as guides for helping you work through the problem. If you can think of any other considerations, go ahead and use them in your approach.

  1. Getting Ready
     a. How do you personally feel about this problem?
     b. What do you know about shoplifting?
     c. Can you develop mental images of someone shoplifting?
     d. What would stores be like if there were no shoplifting?

e. What information do you need to solve this problem?

f. How might you go about collecting this information?

g. What are the major, essential characteristics of the problem?

h. Which characteristics of the problem are related?

i. Which characteristics of the problem are more important than others?

j. Who shoplifts?

k. What do shoplifters steal?

l. Where do people shoplift?

m. When do people shoplift?

n. Why do people shoplift?

2. What's Happening?

a. Can you tune in to the problem to describe in sufficient detail what you would see, hear, touch, taste, or smell in shoplifting situations?

b. Can you vicariously experience the thoughts and feelings of a shoplifter at the moment of taking something?

c. Whats good about shoplifting? In what ways might shoplifting benefit stores and/or other people?

d. Can you imagine the awareness levels of shoplifters, store employees, and customers in the store while a shoplifting act is occurring? How much do they see and hear at this time?

e. What different types of noises, lights, voices, etc. might attract or deter shoplifters?

f. How would you define the problem at this point?

3. Loosening Up Your Mind

a. What are the constraints of this problem?

b. What assumptions do most people make about shoplifters and shoplifting?

c. Can you challenge any of these assumptions? How?

d. What cultural taboos might help shoplifters?

e. What elements of shoplifting are similar to one another? What elements are different?

f. What else is like shoplifting?

g. What reversals can you think of to describe the shoplifting problem?

h. How can you exaggerate the objectives of a shoplifting reduction program?

i. What fantasy solutions to the problem can you develop?

j. What is the silliest possible solution? What practical solution can you develop from this?

k. Look over all your responses. In what ways might you redefine the problem now?

4. Letting Go

a. How many different solutions can you think of in ten minutes?

b. For the moment, forget about the shoplifting problem. In five minutes, how many different ways can you think of to prevent people from doing something? Do any of these ideas suggest possible solutions to the shoplifting problem?

c. Select five different objects from your immediate environment. Giving yourself three minutes for each object, how many different solutions can you think of that might be suggested by the objects?

d. Look over your list of solutions. Can you combine any to produce new solutions?

5. Being Different

a. What makes you mad about shoplifting? In what ways might you change these factors to develop problem solutions?

b. What new names can you think of to describe your solutions to this point? Do these names suggest new solutions?

c. Can you use the different characteristics of a light bulb to suggest possible solutions?

d. Write a brief, one- or two-paragraph story about

shoplifting. Make it silly, if you wish. What new ideas are suggested by this exercise?

e. What is different about your solutions?

f. Can you think of any improvements that could be made on previously tried solutions?

6. You're the Judge

a. What values are relevant to shoplifting incidents?

b. Can you reduce the total number of solutions you have generated to three to five categories? Can you combine any of these solutions?

c. What criteria will your solutions have to satisfy in order to solve the problem?

d. How important are each of these criteria relative to the others?

e. Can you construct a rating chart to help you narrow down your choice of solutions?

f. Which solutions would be most likely to solve the problem?

7. Avoiding Surprises

a. Are there any obstacles to implementation that would be difficult to overcome?

b. What are the worst possible things that could go wrong with your solution?

c. How likely is it that each thing could go wrong; how likely is it that each problem could be prevented?

d. How serious would be the consequences if each thing anticipated went wrong?

e. What might be done to prevent these things from happening?

f. What specific steps will you need to take to implement your solution?

g. What people will have to be persuaded about the worth of your solution?

h. What are the major benefits of your solution?

i. What additional resources will you need for implementation?

j. What new problems are likely to be created by your solution?

k. How could others be rewarded to help you with implementation?

l. What will you need to do to follow up implementation of your solution?

PROBLEM NUMBER TWO

The second problem for you to work on in the applied phase of your program should be a personal problem. It should be a problem you have wanted to resolve, but haven't had the time; or a problem that you have been actively working on, but with little success. In any event, you need to select a problem that you have felt a need to resolve—one that you feel you must solve to reduce some tension within yourself.

Once you have selected this problem, you should begin working on it, using the same questions as guides that you used for the shoplifting problem. Although all of the questions may not apply directly to your problem, you should be able to modify them with little difficulty. Just remember to be flexible in your approach, defer all judgment until you are ready to select a solution, and maintain forward motion during the entire process. Like the first problem, you should allow about two weeks to work on this one—even more if you feel strongly about the problem.

After you have selected one or two possible solutions and have made plans for implementation, you then should attempt to actually implement your solution. If you were working on a problem of some significance to yourself, then you should approach it with the expectation that you can and will solve it. Unless you actually take the final step of putting your solution to work, you will have just gone through the motions in training your mind. Your brain needs feedback, and actually solving a problem is one of the best ways to get this feedback. In doing so, you will be helping yourself to grow further as a creative person—and you should find the experience to be pleasurable as well. There's a lot of truth to the old saying that nothing succeeds like success. So think positively and solve your problem. I know you can do it.

SAMPLE RESPONSES TO THE SHOPLIFTING PROBLEM

Note: The following is presented in a sequential, left-brain manner only to communicate the information more easily. When I actually worked through the problem, I found myself skipping around quite a bit. However, this disjointed activity will not be too apparent from the description.

1. Getting Ready
   a. I feel very upset that people steal merchandise, since the costs are passed on to the consumer. I also feel upset that some people think they have the "right" to shoplift because of inflation and high prices. On the other hand, I feel sorry for poor people who only take clothes for their children.
   b. People shoplift because they are poor, to see if they can get away with it, for the fun of it, because of peer pressure, or because of severe psychological disturbances. Some people have developed elaborate devices (e.g., special boxes with spring doors, coats with pockets sewn on the inside) to aid them; they generally are considered to be professional shoplifters. For other people, the act of shoplifting is more spontaneous. Both employees and customers are guilty of shoplifting. The problem is extremely costly to both stores and customers. Many stores have taken special precautions to thwart shoplifters (e.g., electronic devices, floorwalkers, etc.)
   c. I can see someone casually walk through a store, look around, slip a small item into a pocket, and walk out of the store.
   d. Expensive merchandise would be displayed more openly; there would be no security measures; prices would be lower; store personnel would observe customers less closely.
   e. If what I think I know about shoplifting is fact or

opinion; how many people in a store at a given time are likely to shoplift something; the type of merchandise stolen most frequently; the type of person most likely to be a shoplifter; the time of day and day of week most shoplifting occurs; the reasons most people shoplift, etc.

f. Discussions with store personnel, consultants, journals, and academic publications.

g. The conditions most likely to tempt someone to shoplift; motives; areas of stores that are most susceptible, etc.

h. Perhaps age of shoplifters and time of day (e.g., teenagers after school hours). Would need to do more research to answer this question.

i. Again, I would need to do more research to answer this question.

j. Teenagers, blue-collar workers, white-collar workers, housewives, people from all economic levels.

k. Coats, sweaters, pants, shirts, blouses, rings, necklaces, tools, etc.

l. In all store departments except furniture and large appliances.

m. At all times of the day; when they think they can get away with it.

n. To save money; to punish themselves; to prove something to someone else; to get back at someone else, etc.

2. What's Happening?

a. I can see a lot of people walking around and examining merchandise. There are many different types and sizes of people and a variety of different colors worn by each. I see a lot of glass, metal, and carpeting in the store. There is a constant level of talking, sounds of clothes hangers, and necklaces being placed on glass countertops. The glass is very smooth in places, but sticky in other places from constant touching. My feet walk smoothly over the well-worn carpet. I am surrounded by smells of perfume, body odor, leather, and food in a bakery shop.

b. The clerk has just turned his head so I probably could slip this tie inside my coat. He just looked in my direction, so I'd better be very careful. Maybe if I just turn my back toward him just a little. There. Now I'll check on the clerk one more time. He's busy now, so . . . oops, here comes another customer, but he's more interested in the suits. OK, here goes. I'll just pick it up and quickly stuff it in my coat pocket. I won't even look around while I'm doing it. Now, to just casually walk away from here and out of the store. It sure feels good to have gotten away with that. Why did I do that?

c. One positive feature about shoplifting is that it provides a way for some people to obtain merchandise that they couldn't otherwise afford. It also may be a form of psychological release for some people. Other people might benefit from shoplifting by a feeling of social well-being if they deter a shoplifter or report one to store management; it provides an opportunity for people to do a good deed. Stores might benefit from good customer relations by showing customers that management is concerned about the problem and doesn't want to raise prices unnecessarily.

d. Most customers probably aren't very aware that shoplifting is going on unless they happen to observe it directly and the act is very blatant. The shoplifters themselves will be very tuned in to their environment, pick up many visual and auditory cues that other customers might miss. Store employees are likely to be very aware of the actions of customers, especially those who act suspiciously.

e. A lot of loud talking and low lights probably would be attractive to shoplifters.

f. In what ways might shoplifting by customers be reduced? In what ways might store personnel be more aware of potential shoplifters?

3. Loosening Up Your MInd

a. A major constraint might be to view a solution as requiring that shoplifters be caught in the act. Another constraint might be to view all shoplifters as alike.

b. Most people may view shoplifters as belonging to the lower economic classes; most people may view shoplifting as not being a major problem.

c. I already have challenged these assumptions when I analyzed the problem along other dimensions. I would, however, need to gather data to substantiate my claims.

d. Two taboos would be minding one's own business and not getting involved. Such attitudes would make it much easier to shoplift.

e. Some similar elements would be the need of all shoplifters to avoid being caught, and the fact that most store personnel are trained to watch out for people who may shoplift. Different elements would include such factors as the time of occurrence, the type of merchandise, and the type of shoplifter.

f. Shoplifting is like:

(1) taxes—the consumer always pays a price.

(2) a packrat—higher consumer prices are exchanged for stolen merchandise.

(3) stealing books from a library.

(4) cutting grass—the problem can temporarily be eliminated, but always returns.

g. In what ways might customer shoplifting be increased? In what ways might customers be motivated to give merchandise to the stores? In what ways might shoplifters develop a need to turn themselves in?

h.

Original objective	Stretched objective	Possible solutions
easy to implement	difficult to implement	frisk all customers as they leave the store.
increase profits	decrease profits	give discounts to customers reporting shoplifters.
maintain good customer relations	alienate customers	use qualifying standards to enter the store; start a buying club.

i.

Fantasy solution	Practical solution
Read the minds of all customers.	Develop psychological profiles of shoplifters.
Shoplifted merchandise becomes invisible when taken from store.	Use an exploding dye that is triggered when certain items are removed from a display rack.
A force field prevents shoplifters from entering the store.	Require all coats and packages to be left at the door before entering the store.

j. Ask all customers to please not steal anything. A practical solution would be to develop educational programs in the schools and the local news media.

k. In what ways might:

(1) customers be screened before entering a store?

(2) poor people pay for clothes?

(3) shoplifters be less aware of the store environment?

(4) merchandise be displayed to reduce shoplifting?

(5) subliminal messages be used to discourage shoplifting?

(6) store clerks be trained better to detect shoplifting?

(7) customers help reduce shoplifting?

(8) sounds, lights, textures, colors, or temperature deter shoplifters?

(9) the public be educated better about the shoplifting problem?

(10) more shoplifters be caught in the act?

(11) shoplifters be encouraged to return stolen merchandise?

(12) all customers be frisked before leaving a store?

(Note: All of these redefinitions of the problem actually are subproblems that can be used to suggest possible solutions. The major problem is still preventing the occurrence of shoplifting. However, these problem redefinitions help provide a new perspective on the problem. Any one or all of the redefinitions could be selected to use in generating numerous other solutions.)

4. Letting Go

a. Offer incentives to return stolen merchandise, establish a bartering unit in each store, increase the number of security personnel, use electronic detection devices, put all merchandise in display cses and order by number, have subliminal messages put in store music, offer discounts to customers reporting shoplifters, convert the store into

a buying club with qualifying standards for acceptance, put an electrical field around merchandise that will set off an alarm if tripped, convert to catalog sales, install visible cameras to scan areas of frequent shoplifting, offer free counseling to shoplifters who turn themselves in, stage mock arrests of store employees acting like shoplifters, and have a monthly "shoplifter's day" in which the arrest records of prior shoplifters are made known.
b. Put up a wall, ask them not to do it, physically restrain them, drug them, find out what is rewarding to them and reward them when they don't do it, subject them to peer pressure, lock them in a room, immobilize them, electrically shock them if they try to do it, sit on them, tie them up, educate them with the pros and cons involved, glue them down, make a rule, confuse them, and charge them too much money. From these ideas might come such practical solutions as only allowing people to view merchandise without touching it, offering customer discounts if shoplifting is reduced within a certain time period after they have attended an educational program, paying customers to report shoplifters, and selling only very large, expensive types of merchandise.
c. I have selected a glass, a stapler, a telephone, a plant, and a clock. Glass: Put merchandise in display cases, require customers to ask to see merchandise (like asking for a glass of water), use a one-way mirror on the ceiling from which store personnel can watch customers. Stapler: Put merchandise in boxes which require pushing down on a lever to open. Whenever a lever is pushed down, a light shows on a TV-monitored control station so the customer can be observed inspecting the merchandise, or staple tags to merchandise that must be neutralized electronically before leaving

the store. Otherwise, an alarm will sound. Telephone: Call in to the store to place orders, then pick up at the store; give customers a constantly changing code number that must be dialed before opening a display case or picking up merchandise to inspect it; pick up merchandise in a store by using a telephone receiver connected to a voice-stress analyzer. Anyone whose voice indicates a high stress level must contact a store clerk for assistance. Plant: Sell only expensive merchandise that customers are not allowed to examine without a clerk; use a photoelectric beam which, if broken, sets off an alarm; or have merchandise rigged so that sound vibrations of it being moved outside of store set off an alarm. Clock: Use a timing device that sets off an alarm hidden in the merchandise unless it is turned off before picking up the object; hypnotize all shoplifters, using a ticking sound, so they'll never steal again.

d. Some of the solutions could be combined as follows: Customers apply for a combination credit card and security card that is used to unlock the store, record who has entered, unlock display cases (recording the card number), and make purchases. Another solution would be to offer discounts to customers who attend educational programs on shoplifting.

5. Being Different
a. Shoplifting makes me mad because I have to pay higher prices, I have to put up with security devices and suspicious sales personnel, and because some people think they are entitled to steal due to past injustices done to them. Solutions from this "bug" list might include distributing the price increases due to shoplifting among the shoplifters who are caught, and designing a store in which all potential customers would volunteer to undergo a

security check so that they would not be bothered by security precautions while in the store.

b. Some possible labels for different solutions would be: Catch-a-Crook; Shopping for Shoplifters (customers turning in shoplifters); The Trading Center, Swap It (for a bartering department); Big Brother (for store cameras); Crooked Sounds (for voice-stress analyzer); Your Time Is Up (for timed alarm system); Buy-Safe, You're OK (for credit/security card). No new solutions are suggested to me by these labels.

c. Possible solutions from characteristics of a light bulb include:

(1) screw-action: secure small appliances with screws; have merchandise rotate in a controlled-access display case.

(2) breakable, emits light: to inspect expensive items, a light beam is broken, notifying store personnel.

(3) easily turned on and off: a store clerk turns a switch to permit opening a display case for customer inspection of the merchandise inside.

(4) filament element: tie down merchandise with a nylon line.

d. It's not easy being a shoplifter. Society looks down on you; you're constantly looking over your shoulder. It's especially awkward at cocktail parties when someone introduces you as their friend the shoplifter. You get very little respect.

If more people realized what was involved in becoming a truly competent shoplifter, perhaps more respect would be given to this elite corps. Considerable planning and organizational skills are needed to pull off a successful "lift"—skills that probably rival those of most business executives. An ability to get along with and relate to other people is essential as well. You must be capable of talking your way out of many difficult situations, and it's always nice if you can relate well to your fellow prisoners and the police. The art of shoplifting has been neglected for too long now, and it is time that more recognition is given to this growing profession. Perhaps what is needed most is development of a professional organization complete with its own public relations department. That and an efficient bail-bonding system would go a long way to upgrading the profession.

Possible solutions suggested by this story are: publication of shoplifter arrest records, formation of a local merchants' committee to combat the problem, and "shock" programs in which first-time shoplifters would visit the local jails and talk with police about the consequences of their actions.

e. Although I am not acquainted with all the measures that have been taken to combat shoplifting, I would guess that some of my solutions are different in the following ways: (1) involving other customers to stem the problem, (2) emphasizing rewards for not shoplifting instead of punishment for doing it, (3) restricting access to a considerable variety of merchandise, and (4) the notion of a bartering unit to soften the urge to take something from a store.

f. Many of my proposed solutions are modifications of previous solution attempts or solutions currently in practice. For example, many stores keep small, very expensive items in display cases. Some of the solutions use the display-case concept, but vary in the way access is gained to the cases.

6. You're the Judge

a. The act of shoplifting, its effect on other people, and the shoplifters themselves may reflect such values as justice, equality, self-esteem, security, power, dignity, and honesty. Any decision as to the best solution should incorporate many of these or similar values.

*Figure 11.3 List of Solutions Generated for
the Shoplifting Problem*

---

1. give discounts to customers reporting shoplifters
2. use qualifying standards to enter the store
3. convert stores to a buying club
4. develop psychological profiles of shoplifters
5. use exploding dye on certain items of merchandise
6. require checking of coats and packages at store entrance
7. use subliminal, anti-shoplifting messages in store music
8. train clerks to spot potential shoplifters
9. develop public educational programs for the media
10. offer incentives for return of stolen merchandise
11. establish a bartering unit in each store
12. increase the number of security personnel in the stores
13. install electronic detection devices
14. put all merchandise in controlled-access display cases
15. install an electric field around merchandise
16. convert stores to catalog sales
17. install visible cameras to scan frequent shoplifting areas
18. offer free counseling to shoplifters who turn themselves in
19. stage mock arrests of store personnel posing as shoplifters
20. put on a monthly "Shoplifter's Day" to expose arrest records of prior shoplifters
21. offer discounts to participants in shoplifting educational programs if the incidence of shoplifting is reduced
22. pay money to customers reporting shoplifters
23. sell only large, expensive types of merchandise
24. require customers to ask to see merchandise
25. install a one-way mirror in the ceiling for store personnel to watch customers
26. put merchandise in boxes that require a lever to be

pushed to open the boxes; once the lever is pushed, personnel are alerted on a TV monitor

27. staple tags onto merchandise; the tags must be electronically neutralized before merchandise can be taken out of the store without sounding an alarm

28. assign code numbers to customers to use in opening display cases

29. order merchandise in the store by a phone equipped with a voice-stress analyzer; any indication of anxiety requires assistance of a clerk

30. merchandise above a certain price requires assistance of a clerk

31. install a photo-electric beam above merchandise that sets off an alarm if broken

32. use an alarm that is set off by sound vibrations if merchandise is carried out of the store

33. use a timing device that sets off an alarm hidden in merchandise if not turned off by a clerk

34. hypnotize previous shoplifters so they won't steal again

35. use a combination credit/security card to enter store, unlock display cases, and purchase merchandise; require security check to obtain card

36. spread any price increases arising from shoplifting among convicted shoplifters

37. change store policy so that potential customers must volunteer to undergo a security check to shop without interference of security precautions

38. secure small appliances with screws

39. have merchandise rotate in a controlled-access display case

40. store clerks required to turn switch to open a display case

41. tie down merchandise with nylon lines

42. form a local merchants' committee to study the problem

43. use "shock" probation programs

b. The forty-three solutions generated in the previous stages are presented in Figure 11.3. Using the numbers of these solutions, I have organized them into five categories, as shown in Figure 11.4 (two of the solutions are listed twice, since they overlap into one other category). Among the solutions that could be easily combined would be solutions: 1 and 22; 4 and 8; 18 and 34; 2, 3, 35, and 37; 13, 27, and 32; 14, 15, 24, 26, 28, 29, 31, 33, 35, 38, 39, 40, and 41; 9, 19, 20, 21, 36, 42, and 43.

c. Major criteria might include the cost of the effort, its likelihood of success, ease of implementation, effect on customer relations, time required, effect on sales, and extent to which major physical changes in the store would be required.

d. The criteria could be ranked from highest to lowest importance as follows:
   (1) likelihood of success
   (2) effect on sales
   (3) cost
   (4) effect on customer relations
   (5) time required
   (6) physical changes required
   (7) ease of implementation

e. To illustrate construction of this chart, a one- to five-point rating scale is used to evaluate the five solution categories described in Figure 11.4. (For more information on how to construct such a chart, review exercise 9.05, Weigh-In.)

Figure 11.4   Categorization of Shoplifting Problem Solutions

Category	Solution Number
I. Customer involvement	1, 22
II. Psychological aspects of shoplifting	4, 7, 8, 10, 11, 17, 18, 34
III. Keep shoplifters out of the store	2, 3, 16, 35, 37
IV. Make shoplifting difficult/ prevent from leaving the store	5, 6, 12, 13, 14, 15, 17, 23, 24, 25, 26, 27, 28, 29, 30, 31, 32, 33, 35, 38, 39, 40, 41
V. Educational efforts	9, 19, 20, 21, 36, 42, 43

		Satisfaction				
Criteria	Impor-tance	I	II	III	IV	V
success	5	3 15	3 15	5 25	5 25	1 5
sales	5	2 10	4 20	4 20	5 25	1 5
cost	4	4 16	1 4	2 8	1 4	3 12
customer relations	4	5 20	3 12	1 4	1 4	5 20
time	3	3 9	2 6	1 3	2 6	2 6
physical changes	3	5 15	2 6	3 9	2 6	1 3
implemen-tation	2	4 8	3 6	2 4	1 2	2 4
		93	69	73	72	55

f. Based on these ratings, the solutions in the customer-involvement category (I) would be most likely to solve the problem, while educational efforts (Category V) would be least likely to stem the incidence of shoplifting. As constructed, this chart represents a shortcut to the overall evaluation process. To be more thorough, the solution combinations within each category should be subjected to the same procedure. The highest-rated solutions within the categories then might be combined with some solutions from other categories to define the final approach to the problem.

7. Avoiding Surprises

For purposes of illustration, the customer-involvement solutions will be used to respond to the questions in this section.

a. One major obstacle would be overcoming a social taboo on reporting the misdeeds of other people. Another obstacle would be the difficulty involved in establishing the validity of shoplifting claims made by one customer against another.

Questions *b.* through *e.* can be responded to best by constructing a chart of potential problems, preventive actions, and ratings of the likelihood (L) and seriousness of occurrence (S) of the problems (1 = not very likely, 5= very likely; 1= not very serious, 5 = very serious).

Problems	L	S	*Preventive Actions*
Unjust accusations	4	5	Develop clear guidelines; mail literature to customers.
Court cases require customer presence	2	3	Use depositions.
Reluctance to accuse others of shoplifting	4	5	Use educational programs and financial incentives.

Problems	L	S	Preventive Actions
Shoplifters seek vengeance against accusers	2	5	Use an anonymous reporting procedure; guarantee confidentiality.

f. Some of the major implementation steps would include promotional mailings to customers and newspaper articles to acquaint people with the proposed program, conducting a survey to define the amount of interest in the program, consultations with legal counsel, discussions with company financial personnel regarding the amount of financial investments involved and likely return on investments, development of program brochures, development of program policies, and planning the promotional activities.

g. All current and potential customers, all management personnel, and those persons who would be directly involved with the legal and financial aspects of the program.

h. Perhaps the greatest benefit to be expected from this program would be its value as a public-relations and educational device. The program would show customers that the store is concerned about the problem and is interested in holding down prices. In addition, the program would help to educate the public about the seriousness and pervasiveness of the problem. Of course, the final outcome should be a slight increase in profits for the store.

i. Time will be the major resource needed to implement and carry through the program. The initial financial costs most likely can be written off against the eventual increase in gains due to less shoplifting.

j. In addition to some of the problems discussed previously, a major problem could be an initial mobbing of the store as people try to spot shoplifters. Some violations of individual rights could occur during the start-up phase. Some problem-solving efforts will be required to deal with these problems.

k. Customers will be rewarded financially and perhaps by a sense of well-being in helping deal with a social problem. Store personnel will be rewarded by the expectation of increased sales (more customers should come to the store) and profits.

l. The major follow-up activities will be making provisions for handling any court cases that might arise, adjudicating disputes among customers, continued training of store personnel (especially clerks), continued promotion of the program, reporting of the results to the public, and close monitoring of the program, especially during the early stages.

BIBLIOGRAPHY AND REFERENCES

Adams, J. L. *Conceptual Blockbusting*, 2nd ed. New York: W. W. Norton & Company, 1979.

Albrecht, K. *Brain Power.* Englewood Cliffs, N.J.: Prentice-Hall, Inc., 1980.

Anderson, B. F. *The Complete Thinker.* Englewood Cliffs, N.J.: Prentice-Hall, Inc., 1980.

Brightman, H. J. *Problem Solving: A Logical and Creative Approach.* Atlanta: College of Business Administration, Georgia State University, 1980.

Campbell, D. *Take the Road to Creativity and Get Off Your Dead End.* Niles, Ill.: Argus Communications, 1977.

Edwards, B. *Drawing on the Right Side of the Brain.* Los Angeles: J. P. Tarcher, Inc., 1979.

Elijah, A. M. *Thinking Unlimited.* Pune, India: Institute of Creative Development, 1980.

Hanks, K., L. Belliston, and D. Edwards. *Design Yourself!* Los Altos, Calif.: William Kaufmann, Inc., 1978.

Hermann, W. E. *The Hermann Brain Dominance Instrument.* Stamford, Conn.: Applied Creative Services, 1980.

Jacobson, E. *Progressive Relaxation.* Chicago: The University of Chicago Press, Midway Reprint, 1974.

Kirst, W., and U. Diekmeyer. *Creativity Training.* New York: Peter H. Wyden, Inc., 1973.

Koberg, D., and J. Bagnall. *The Universal Traveler.* Los Altos, Calif.: William Kaufmann, Inc., 1976.

Loch, C. "How to feed your brain and develop your creativity." *Writer's Digest* (February 1981), pp. 20–28.

Lynch, D. "The case for disorderly conduct: How to get the most out of managerial manpower." *Management Review* (February 1980), pp. 15–19.

Lynch, D. "It's time we give the brain its due." *Journal of Organizational Communication* 1 (1981), pp. 8–10.

Olson, R. W. *The Art of Creative Thinking.* New York: Barnes & Noble, 1980.

Prince, G. "Putting the other half of the brain to work." *Training* (November 1978), pp. 57–58; 60–61.

Raudsepp, E. (with G. P. Hough, Jr.). *Creative Growth Games.* New York: Jove Publications, Inc., 1977.

Raudsepp, E. *More Creative Growth Games.* New York: Perigee Books, 1980.

Raudsepp, E. "How creative are you?" In *Dun's Review,* "Business probes the creative spark" (January 1980), pp. 32–38.

Samuels, M., and N. Samuels. *Seeing With the Mind's Eye.* New York: Random House, Inc., 1975.

Simberg, A. L. *Creativity at Work.* Boston: Industrial Education Institute, 1964.

Torrance, E. P. *The Torrance Tests of Creative Thinking.* Lexington, Mass.: Personnel Press/Ginn, 1974.

VanGundy, A. B. *Techniques of Structured Problem Solving.* New York: Van Nostrand Reinhold, 1981.

INDEX